WOMEN
IN
TRANSITION

WOMEN
IN
TRANSITION

By

ANDREW J. DuBRIN, Ph.D.

Associate Professor
College of Business
Rochester Institute of Technology
Rochester, New York

CHARLES C THOMAS · PUBLISHER
Springfield · *Illinois* · *U.S.A.*

Published and Distributed Throughout the World by
CHARLES C THOMAS · PUBLISHER
BANNERSTONE HOUSE
301-327 East Lawrence Avenue, Springfield, Illinois, U.S.A.
NATCHEZ PLANTATION HOUSE
735 North Atlantic Boulevard, Fort Lauderdale, Florida, U.S.A.

© *1972, by* CHARLES C THOMAS · PUBLISHER
ISBN 0-398-02273-9 (cloth)
ISBN 0-398-02485-5 (paper)
Library of Congress Catalog Card Number: 74-180811

With THOMAS BOOKS *careful attention is given to all details of manufacturing and design. It is the Publisher's desire to present books that are satisfactory as to their physical qualities and artistic possibilities and appropriate for their particular use.* THOMAS BOOKS *will be true to those laws of quality that assure a good name and good will.*

Printed in the United States of America
Y-2

In memory of my mother
Louise Walsh DuBrin

PREFACE

This book is written for homemakers who want to psychologically grow as people. It provides a variety of constructive suggestions on how to make the transition from discontentment to a more rewarding life. The dilemma of the housewife who finds some aspects of her life stultifying is not a revelation happened upon by this author. Much has been written about the housewife syndrome. Even the women's liberation movement owes much of its impetus to the discontents of women who feel trapped as homemakers.

After personally observing and reading about some of the problems of women, it occurred to me that more could be done to help homemakers with their problems. This book reflects such an attempt.

All of what we have to say is not new. Educators, pyschologists, vocational counselors, psychiatrists, and a variety of professional writers have devoted effort to improving the satisfactions (or decreasing the frustrations of) housewives. Here we bring together many of these approaches in such a way that a transition from distress to enrichment will appear feasible.

Many people have contributed directly and indirectly to the preparation of this book. Appreciation is due Joyce Raymond DuBrin for her suggestion that I write a book about the problems of women. Although she may not necessarily agree with all of the thoughts expressed in this book, many of her ideas about people are reflected in my writings. Approximately 150 of my students conducted field research with a total of 600 women in conjunction with this project.

Thanks are due Drs. Eugene Fram and Francena Miller and Miss Marion Grover, all of the Rochester Institute of Technology, for both their ideas about the problems of women and their encouragement. Dr. Laurence Lipsett of R.I.T. and Mrs. Priscilla Jackson of Oakland University made valuable information from their files available to me. The women I personally interviewed in the conduct of my research also receive my appreciation. Dean Jerry Young and Mrs. Lillyan Fahy are due thanks for providing organizational support to this project.

Many of the ideas contained in this book have been gathered from newspapers, magazine articles, and other books. Hopefully I have given appropriate credit to these sources by the use of footnotes. To any instances of unwitting plagiarism I plead guilty.

Miss Joanne Szczepanski, who has now typed two books for me, receives my deepest appreciation. Joanne performed superbly as a manuscript typist, and her reactions to my ideas were heartwarming.

ANDREW J. DuBRIN

CONTENTS

WOMEN
IN
TRANSITION

Chapter 1

THE HOUSEWIFE SYNDROME

> . . . *We can no longer ignore that voice within women that says: "I want something more than my husband and my children and my home."*
>
> BETTY FRIEDAN
> *The Feminine Mystique**

What Is the Housewife Syndrome?

SELF-DOUBT, self-pity, and discontentment are familiar feelings to about one third of American housewives. Most of these women exhibit behavior patterns well within the normal range and their personal conflicts and fantasies are shared by many other women. Dismissing these women as neurotic, malcontented, or unappreciative oversimplifies the problem. The phenomenon of the dissatisfied middle class housewife is so ubiquitous that a label has emerged to describe this malady of the normal woman—the "housewife syndrome." The specific form of the housewife syndrome is slightly different for each woman, but each case is similar enough to justify the technical term "syndrome." (Syndromes are groups of symptoms or signs that occur together and characterize a disease, disorder, or pattern of behavior.) Characteristic symptoms of the housewife syndrome are generalized feelings of discontent, recognition that one's capacities are underutilized, fatigue, apathy, boredom, lethargy, and guilt about having these feelings. Occasionally, to escape these feelings, fantasy enters the picture. More generally stated, the houswife syndrome is a collection of unpleasant feelings and emotions precipitated by occupying

**The Feminine Mystique* by Betty Friedan. Copyright © 1963 by Betty Friedan, W.W. Norton & Company, Inc., New York, New York.

the role of a housewife. Mentally ill women may experience this syndrome in addition to their other conflicts, but women who experience the housewife syndrome are not necessarily mentally ill.

Middle class housewives experience the syndrome in higher proportion than do those of upper or lower class. Upper class women have the financial wherewithal to circumvent some of the homemaker's sources of boredom and frustration. Lower class women infrequently experience the housewife syndrome because their expectations in life are set sufficiently low to avoid disappointment. Their psychological demands thus are less than those of middle and upper middle class women.

Norma Gorbaty is a thirty-one-year-old college-educated woman with two preschool-age children. She lives in the suburbs, attends weekly meetings of a local bridge club, and sporadically participates in charity drives. Norma's husband is a chemical engineering supervisor. She does not work outside the home. The frustrations and dissatisfactions Norma experiences in her role illustrate the housewife syndrome:

> Face it, I have a lot of hang-ups about my life as a housewife. First of all, how can you call this work I do a job? There is no room for advancement in my position. I'm not learning anything new. Why did I bother going to college? Maids, servants, and average people could do most of my job as well as I can. My kids are great but they are not mentally stimulating. When I get behind in my ironing or washing or sewing I become more and more lazy. Sometimes I feel drugged. I drink too much coffee, I smoke too many cigarettes, and my friends and I are beginning to have cocktails at three in the afternoon. I know it's all because I'm a housewife. I'm not looking to leave my marriage, but I will try and convince my daughter not to get married right after college. It's a waste of talent.[1]

Estimates of the proportion of women experiencing these feelings have shown consistency over the last decade. Margaret Mead conservatively estimated more than ten years ago that over one quarter of women in the United States are "definitely disturbed" about their lot as women. Furthermore, as alluded to earlier, the proportion of dissatisfied women is higher among the ". . . middle class pace setters who are the most favored and emancipated."[2] Results of a Gallup poll in the summer of 1970 (when women's liberation activity was particularly high) indicated that 35 percent of women felt that women in the United States do not get as good a break as men. My research with six hundred housewives in New York State suggested that about 30 percent of these women manifested significant dissatisfaction with the homemaker role. It appears more than coincidental that studies of job satisfaction among a variety of occupational groups indicate that about 35 percent of personnel are dissatisfied with their jobs. Homemakers and many other occupational groups experience the same proportion of discontented members.

Several other terms have been used to characterize the same phenomenon as the housewife syndrome: "housewife's blight," "cabin fever," and "the problem that has no name."[3] All these conditions are characterized by basic symptoms such as feelings of lack of accomplishment, fatigue, and guilt. Housewife's blight adds a new dimension to the problem. Under this condition women manifest bleeding blisters on the hands and arm. The housewife syndrome thus has potential psychosomatic manifestations. Whatever the name given to this predicament faced by some housewives, it is characterized by the major symptoms of feelings of underaccomplishment, fatigue, and guilt.

Feelings of underaccomplishment (or feelings of lack of self-fulfillment) underlie perhaps every situation of the housewife syndrome. Any person placed in a role where their skills and capacities far exceed those demanded by the job will experience some degree of frustration. During a recession it is not uncommon for physicists to work as laboratory technicians, nor for engineers to work as draftsmen. These people will begin to notice that their needs for accomplishment and recognition are thwarted once their more urgent needs for short-range income have been satisfied. Similarly housewives who feel that the demands of their basic role in life do not tap close to their full potential as human beings will experience pangs of thwarted psychological growth.

Personality theorists have maintained for over thirty years that most normal—nonpathological nor immature—people are motivated by desires for self-actualization. Simply stated, the need for self-actualization is the drive to become what one is capable of becoming. To the extent that a person can feel that his or her potentials are being fully tapped, a feeling of self-satisfaction emerges. Most aspects of homemaking do not stretch the creative potentials of normal women. Few roles in life provide continuous opportunities to gratify desires for self-actualization. However, the problem is particularly acute for homemakers because so many tasks confronting the homemaker are trivial in nature. Women in our study fully recognize that there are different facets or components to the homemaker role. Tasks such as washing, ironing, floor mopping, and closet cleaning frequently have a negative psychological impact upon women. Entertaining, gourmet cooking, conferring with children about their problems, and providing advice and counsel to husbands are examples of activities inherent in the housewife role that provide more opportunity for the satisfaction of higher-level needs. Later in this chapter the multi-faceted nature of the housewife's role will be examined in more depth.

Full-time homemaking frustrates the needs for accomplishment of some women more than others. Women with limited potential to handle creative or self-actualizing work find all the intellectual challenge they desire in the homemaker role. Women motivated by thoughts of establishing a career for themselves outside the home but whose present life situation does not permit pursuing a career are particularly frustrated. Many other women do not fall prey to feelings of lack of self-fulfillment by developing a life plan that integrates homemaking tasks with other more psychologically rewarding activities. These fortunate individuals are women who have made the transition this book is about.

Fatigue, boredom, apathy, and indifference are closely related characteristics of the housewife syndrome. For example, bored people are readily fatigued and fatigued people are readily bored. Fatigue associated with the housewife syndrome is more frequently *psychological* than *physiological* in origin. Physiological fatigue is an actual impairment in ability to perform a task, resulting from physical exertion. Waste products such as lactic acid accumulate because of prolonged physical exertion. Some tasks required of homemakers, such as floor scrubbing, if carried out for prolonged stretches can result in genuine physiological fatigue. The homemaker's body is reduced in its capacity to perform more physical work as a result of strenuous physical activity. Psychological fatigue is more subtle in origin. Psychiatrists, gynecologists, and psychologists have concluded that most instances of fatigue generated by the homemaking function are partially, if not completely, psychological in origin.

Boredom, the primary symbol of psychological fatigue, is a feeling usually associated with work that is intrinsically uninteresting to the individual in question. To the extent that a homemaker finds homemaking uninteresting she will experience boredom and fatigue. This boredom further manifests itself in attitudes of apathy and indifference.

Generalized feelings of discontent, or "moodyness," can also be symptomatic of the housewife syndrome. The housewife directs her discontent toward people, objects, or situations that are not directly related to the cause of her discontentment. "Displacement" is the technical term for this defense mechanism. Sufferers of the housewife syndrome can be difficult people to live with because their moods are unpredictable. Children are often used as scapegoats toward whom the discontented homemaker directs her anger. The woman might be dissatisfied with herself for disliking many aspects of her role in life; however, it is less anxiety-producing to be mad at children than at oneself.

Feelings of discontentment also manifest themselves in the form of "lowered frustration tolerance." Because the homemaker cannot gratify many of her higher-level needs, her toleration for any further frustration is lowered. People angry at themselves become angry at other people upon minor provocation. Husbands have commented to me that their wives were more pleasant to live with once they (the wives) found more satisfying jobs, hobbies, or educational courses. Proponents of women's liberation have argued that once women are liberated, men will also benefit because liberated women are more pleasant and interesting companions. Conversely, discontented women who feel that their role in life is unsatisfactory can be unpleasant and uninteresting companions. The popular notion that "bored women are boring" is an accurate generalization.

Repetitive work contributes to feelings of boredom and psychological fatigue among industrial and business workers. Housework has many repetitive elements. Work accomplished today, particularly cleaning tasks, quickly becomes undone and must be repeated. Boredom has several undesirable side effects. Besides becoming disenchanted with the activity she finds boring, the homemaker may develop more generalized feelings of apathy and indifference. This leads to a reluctance or unwillingness to attempt activities that might lead to greater need satisfaction. One woman, asked about her plans to overcome the frustrations in her life, responded, "I think that's part of my problem. With three children running around under foot, I'm so busy I can't get into anything interesting or mentally challenging. My basic life is so boring that I can't get up enough energy to try new things."

Fatigue and boredom have such a profound negative impact upon female sexual adjustment that this problem has long been the topic of many jokes. Men may look toward sexual relations with their spouse as a pleasant way to relieve feelings of boredom and monotony. Women, in contrast, frequently are drawn away from sexual activity with their husbands because of boredom and fatigue stemming from other matters. The oft-repeated female defense against intercourse, "I'm just too tired tonight," may in reality mean: "My life experiences are so stultifying that a generalized feeling of fatigue and boredom have inhibited my sexuality. Catch me when life looks a little better to me."

Guilt feelings represent a covert, almost unconscious symptom of the housewife syndrome. Her feelings of guilt may stem from several origins. First, the housewife feels guilty about not being completely content in her role as wife and mother. Second, she feels guilty about feeling that an important part of her capabilities are not being used. Third, the housewife may feel guilty about neglecting her children when she finally embarks upon a program of self-development. H. Gray, a clinical psychiatrist, contends that feelings of guilt over imagined or actual child neglect is one of the most common anxieties leading women to psychotherapy.[4] All three sources of guilt were noted in the late 1950's and early 1960's. Cultural values may have changed sufficiently since then to suggest that guilt over devoting time to oneself or not being content with the housewife role is less prevalent today. Guilt per se is a nonconstructive emotion. In contrast, guilt that motivates a woman to seek a satisfying role in life is a constructive emotion.

Fantasy is yet another significant symptom of the housewife syndrome. It may be classified as a symptom of the syndrome, or as an attempt to cope with (or escape from) the daily frustrations of a housewife. Margaret Reynolds, the housewife-heroine of *Up the*

Sandbox, copes with her situation of the housewife syndrome by

> . . . alternating between reality and dreams of glory that Mitty
> would be proud to claim. Her hours watching her offspring in the
> playground are brief respites from harrowing trips to Viet Nam and
> nights interviewing Fidel Castro as America's star female reporter.
> By day she extols the virtues of the grocery list as pop art. By night
> she is an intern working miracles in a ghetto hospital . . .[5]

This illustration from fiction illuminates an important characteristic of the housewife syndrome. Women experiencing these feelings are looking toward roles in life that will make better use of their potential. Many women, even those with stimulating hobbies and careers, have sexual fantasies. Recent data suggests that for women to fantasize about having sexual relations with another man (or men) during intercourse with their husbands is within the normal range. Career success is not designed to eliminate these fantasies and not all fantasies are attributable to the housewife syndrome.

To understand what factors are responsible for bringing about, causing, or precipitating the housewife syndrome, it is important to first examine the complexity of "occupation: housewife."

The Housewife Role Is Complex

Many women find the term "housewife" objectionable. Asked their opinion about a suitable alternative, the responses are meager. "Homemaker" and "domestic engineer" are the two most frequently given alternatives, with the former—homemaker—offered more seriously than the latter. No one term suitably describes what a housewife does. Full-time homemakers occupy a minimum of three roles: housekeeper, mother, and wife. Much of the housewife syndrome is attributable to the housekeeper and mother roles. Dislike for the wife role, combined with a strong liking for the mother and homemaker role, indicates poor marital adjustment, not the housewife syndrome. These three roles show some overlap. For example, being a wife implies that some routine, tedious chores will have to be performed for the husband. Another approach to classifying the housewife role is to distinguish between the interpersonal and production functions. Helping children with their homework illustrates an interpersonal function, while shampooing the rug is a production function.

Further understanding of the complexity of the housewife's role is found in an analysis provided by P.H. Taylor. Five categories are used to classify the housewife's many functions and activities in Taylor's scheme:

> Exercise of Skills—activities such as cooking, sewing, nursing, gardening and decorating.
>
> Family Organization—planning schedules, budgeting, and creating a sound environment which works well.
>
> Love and Affection—functions such as being responsive to the emotional needs of husbands and children, providing emotional security, love and warmth.
>
> Maintenance of Self—activities concerned with one's own intellectual and emotional identity such as taking an adult education course, or yoga.
>
> Social Relationships—these include contacts with relatives, friendships, interaction with neighbors, entertaining friends and business acquaintances of the husband's.[6]

Frequently the homemaker simultaneously carries out activities that belong to more than one of these categories. Entertaining guests, as one case in point, is a "Social Relationship" activity but also requires "Exercise of Skills" such as cooking and decorating.

Annabelle Bender Motz prepared an intriguing analysis of the difference between the middle class, educated woman's role and the scientist's role.[7] Her analysis was designed to demonstrate conflict between the scientist and housewife roles for the woman who attempts to shift back and forth between both. This analysis can be applied to the different facets of a housewife's role, thus providing additional understanding about the problems of homemakers. It is precisely these problems that contribute to, or constitute part of, the housewife syndrome.

Clarity of the Role. The scientist's role is relatively clear-cut. It is an occupational role for which the person receives financial remuneration when certain tasks or assignments are performed. Other roles are subsidiary to the central role of the scientist. The middle class housewife's role definition is ambiguous; she is not supposed to be primarily a housewife, mother, or committee member. Remuneration for this role is at best indirect. Similar to the scientist role, the housewife role is a central role to which other roles are subsidiary.

Voluntary versus Involuntary. People voluntarily assume the scientist's role. The person is "called"—or chooses science as a way of life. Scientists go through a prolonged period of preparation for the role. In contrast, the housewife role is semivoluntary. The woman may "choose" to marry or to have children. Her choice of one part of the role necessitates that she assume other parts of the role. Strong cultural pressures still exist for married woman to have children and for women with children to be married—particularly among middle class people.

Ego Involvement. The scientist is emotionally involved in his or her work, but emotional expression must be controlled. Extreme objectivity is called for. Scientists must be able to postpone pleasure and anticipate some frustration. Housewives experience intense emotional involvement and relatively free expression of emotions. Attempts are made to avert frustration. Adaptability is required on the part of the housewife to meet the demands of family and friends. Effective housewives are flexible people.

Nature of Activity. Scientists perform mental rather than physical work. Logic and rationality characterize scientific activity. There is a strain for an idea, for creativity, and for originality. There is a desire to contribute facts that serve as a basis for future knowledge. Results of a scientist's work are submitted to an outside world (e.g. scientific journals) that will provide an impersonal appraisal of one's work.

Mental and physical activity are both necessary in the housewife roles. There is little specific goal direction to the mental activity. Activities must be performed within a circumscribed period of time. The housewife is preoccupied with trivia in comparison to the concerns of the scientist.

Degree of Specialization. Scientists work in highly specialized fields. The scientist tries to find out about a minute part of nature and become an authority on this topic. Graduate students, for example, have suggested that the purpose of a doctoral dissertation is for the candidate to learn "more and more about less and less." The housewife is a classic example of a generalist. She must perform in part the functions of a cook, bartender, lover, nursemaid, nurse, hostess, bookkeeper, chauffeur, referee, child therapist, and laundress. Minimal training is required for the housewife role, yet some knowledge of many different jobs is expected. Housewives are rarely viewed as expert on any one function. Even expertise in cooking, for example, is seen as more characteristic of a chef than a housewife.

Social Status. Scientists occupy a relatively high status in society, although sometimes they are perceived as eccentric. Higher status is afforded scientists by middle and upper class than by lower class groups. The scientist is recognized as an important contributor to the high standard of living in modern industrial nations. Housewives in most western nations suffer from low status, aside from the status they receive because of the achievements of their husband. Asked what they do, many housewives respond, "just a housewife" or "not working." The housewife is considered dispensable because specialists can perform her function. Widowers, for example, replace with domestic help many of the functions their wives performed. No monetary evaluation is generally assigned her skills which would provide a basis for elevating the status of a housewife.

Chong Soo Pyun, an economist, attempted recently to establish the monetary value of a housewife. This monetary figure was derived to establish the value of a forty-one-year-old housewife with three adolescent sons. She was a liberal arts college graduate, not gainfully employed, and lived in the eastern United States. Pyun's elaborate statistical analysis suggested that the total replacement cost for an eleven-year period would be $105,000.[8] Housewives, according to this economic analysis, have the same market value as skilled workers. It is the rare skilled worker, however, who will duplicate all of the wife's functions even at the threat of dismissal.

What Causes the Housewife Syndrome?

Symptoms and causes are often difficult to separate; one can appear indistinguishable from another. This confusion occurs even at a physiological level. Parents often state that their children are sick because they have fevers, while the reverse is more nearly correct. Children have fevers because they are sick; a fever forms as a defense against a foreign infection. Similarly, does lack of accomplishment cause the housewife syndrome, or are feelings of a lack of accomplishment merely a symptom? This part of our chapter examines six factors that are more nearly causes than symptoms of the housewife syndrome. The comparison between the scientist and housewife roles just presented hints at much of our analysis of causes.

Rising Expectations of Women

Multiple pressures exist today for women to demand more satisfying and fulfilling role in life. Women's liberation, for example, is a continuous reminder to women that they are entitled to more fulfilling experiences in life than the execution of household chores. Proportionally few women are active liberationists, yet feminists have planted seeds of discontent in many women who were not particularly disturbed by their housewife role. Contentment with a conventional homemaker role is perceived either as old-fashioned or as submission to male chauvinism by feminists. Many college-age women contend they even reject marriage as a satisfactory life style.

Educational levels of women in the United States continue to rise, suggesting that the proportion of women dissatisfied with full-time homemaking will increase. According to Lewis, the proportion of all girls between eighteen and twenty-one who are enrolled in college has risen steadily during this century to a current level of 25 percent.[9] (Some writers argue that women in the United States were less interested in formal education in the 1960's than they were in the 1920's. Correctly observed was the fact that the proportion of women among all college students has been declining for many years from a peak of 47 percent in 1920. The ratio of women to men reached a low of 30 percent in 1950. By 1964 the proportion was 39 percent and may be higher today. Underlying this was the fact that increasingly larger proportions of men attended college. More women were attending college, but men were attending college at an even faster rate of increase. Women were neither losing interest in college, nor were they facing increasing amounts of antifemale prejudice.)

Women's expectations about the breadth and depth of their psychological satisfactions will rise because of an even broader sociological fact. More and more people are demanding more and more material and psychic rewards. The performance of household chores and the lack of involvement in the world outside the home will thus precipitate housewife-syndrome-type complaints from an increasing proportion of women. Factory workers, school teachers, professional athletes, and homemakers anticipate greater satisfactions from their respective roles in society.

Isolation from People

Homemaking can be a lonely existence for women with strong needs for affiliation with other adults. Homemaking tasks such as ironing, washing, and shopping can be more efficiently performed without rather than with the accompaniment of other adults. Interaction with adults in these situations actually hampers the work output of the homemaker. In most occupations interaction with people is a normal part of the job; rest breaks do not have to be scheduled in order to converse with other adults. Bank tellers, bus drivers, lawyers, high school teachers, and psychiatrists all have social intercourse in the usual conduct of their responsibilities. Homemakers, in contrast, often resort to small informal coffee groups to counteract the social isolation in their daily activities. Winter time in northern climates intensifies feelings of isolation and desolateness, because women spend even less time out-of-doors in contact with people. Comparisons have been drawn between feelings of prisoners and homemakers with respect to social isolation. As stated by Edwin C. Lewis: ". . . The feeling that the four walls have become a prison is especially prevalent among young mothers, whose mobility is severely restricted by their responsibilities to their children. These women are truly in danger of going 'stir crazy.' "[10]

Changes in the family structure have contributed to the present-day feeling of social isolation experienced by housewives. Nuclear families have gradually replaced larger, more complex family units. Children, less so than in the past, are raised primarily by their mothers and fathers. The gradual disappearance of the large family is much more prevalent in suburbs than in central cities. Ghettos, ethnic villages, and "old-fashioned" neighborhoods have some limitations, but they offer one antidote to social isolation. Multitudes of family members and neighbors live in close physical proximity. Child rearing and the conduct of homemaking chores thus do not bring about feelings of isolation. It has been reasoned that women were better adjusted psychologically when they washed clothes in the river in a group setting. Housewives of primitive times at least had frequent social interaction.

Mechanization of the homemaking task also contributes to the housewife's isolation. Washing machines, as just suggested, have become sociologically imperfect devices. Launderettes helped alleviate feelings of social isolation. Women came together for the socially acceptable purpose of clothes washing and could devote the thirty-minute waiting time to informal interaction. Once washing machines were installed in most homes, this gave women one less mandatory reason for socializing with one another. Shopping by telephone is another advance of automation that contributes to feelings of social isolation. Physical movement from one neighborhood store to another may be inefficient, but it is less lonely than shopping by telephone.

Women who have worked outside the home and then become full-time homemakers are especially vulnerable to feelings of social isolation. Women who enjoyed high career satisfaction in the past feel most acutely the social isolation. One housewife with three children who was formerly employed as a bookkeeper mentioned, "I used to be really bothered by not having a 'real adult' to talk to during the day. It got so bad I worked out a plan with my husband. He now comes home for lunch three days a week, and at least that problem is taken care of."

Absence of "real adults" to interact with during the day has another subtle deleterious effect upon a woman's psychological well-being. Clifford Kirkpatrick notes that exclusive contact with children day after day may cause otherwise mature women to regress to a childhood level.[11] Symptoms may range from baby talk to concentration on the obvious and to sharing with children a childlike dependence upon the husband.

Philip E. Slater, a sociologist, contends that feelings of social isolation can only be overcome by a sense of community.[12] This sense of community no longer exists in modern neighborhoods, nor do conventional living arrangements provide a sense of community. To achieve this feeling of group living some women consciously or unconsciously raise large families. Children, of course, are only partial solutions to the need for adult companionship and intellectual stimulation. Establishing meaningful patterns of social intercourse outside the home represents the most direct solution to the social isolation of the homemaker.

Constant Interruptions

Homemakers with young children often lead disrupted, hectic, disorganized, and unplanned days. Unless a woman is particularly skillful at planning and budgeting time she can devote much of her day to wasted motion. Some homemakers cram all their housekeeping and self-development activities into periods when the children are napping or sleeping. This unfortunately makes for an unusually long day. Women with young children have commented that they only read magazine articles that are two or three pages in length or books with brief chapters. This selection of reading material by length is done to adjust for the brief episodes of time available for reading without interruption.

Executives, physicians, and housewives share one common experience. Utilization of their time is determined to a large extent by the demands of other people. Mother's role, as perceived by her children and often her husband, is to satisfy their needs. Husbands ask for help in packing for a business trip, and children demand immediate attention when their knees are scraped, or if their cub scout uniform needs ironing for tomorrow's den meeting. These demands are unpredictable and aperiodic. The ultimate tragedy of the interrupted housewife is exemplified by the homemaker who in therapy exclaimed, "Jesus Christ, last night my kid called for a drink of water just when I was on the verge of having an orgasm. My husband laughed, but it ruined the evening for me." Unlike the executive, there is no time when a homemaker can close the office and leave behind the demands of her occupational role.

Psychological research has shown that incompleted activities leave behind a residual of tension which serves as a reminder that a given task has not been completed. Many of the homemaker's tasks fall into the category of *incompleted tasks*, suggesting another cause of frustration in her life. Magazine articles half read, buttons never sewn, poems begun but left to gather dust, and letters to friends never answered are familiar manifestations of the disrupted routine of many homemakers. Time for oneself is a precious commodity during the years of raising preschool children. This situation dramatically reverses itself once children are no longer home during the day. Women then confront the problem of finding meaningful ways to fill their time. Betty Friedan has observed that women who have both career and home responsibilities are very efficient homemakers.[13] They accomplish as many homemaking tasks as do full-time homemakers in perhaps one third the time. Homemaking can expand to fill the time available when life presents no meaningful alternatives to homemaking.

Housewives Have Low Status

Were an industrial psychologist asked to suggest a positive way to frustrate or demotivate a capable individual, he would probably reply, "Place that person in an occupation afforded low status by society, and keep him involved in tasks well below his skill level." For many women the basic job of the homemaker fits such a disheartening situation. Housekeeping, much more than child-rearing or husband-tending functions, involves low status. Occupations centering around child care or child rearing generally provide average or above average social status to their members. Pediatricians, pediatriac nurses, elementary school teachers, and child psychologists enjoy satisfactory status. Mistresses, geisha girls, and call girls receive medium-level status. Domestic servants, janitors, and cleaning women, however, rest on the bottom rung of the status ladder. Janitorial tasks figure prominently in the daily routine of the homemaker. One suburban housewife who ran a well-managed, carefully cleaned home, lamented, "Sure I do a good job as a homemaker, but any dumb broad can do the same thing."

Reliable domestic help, upper middle income women contend, is becoming increasingly scarce. Basic economic and sociological facts underlie this social change. Potential household maids look for work which pays higher and has more prestige. Basic factory jobs, such as assembling parts, pay better and have more status than does domestic work.

Priscilla Jackson, an active participant in helping women establish more meaningful lives for themselves, comments that the status of homemaking has shown a gradual decline.[14] Earlier in history homemakers were called upon to exercise a variety of difficult skills. Homemakers, in greater proportion than they do today, designed their own clothing and draperies. Fewer prepared meals were available, thus calling for more culinary artistry on the woman's part. Women in the past perhaps played an even more important role in the education and training of their children. Nursery schools and kindergartens were fewer in number and less widely used. Opportunities to express the *craftsman instinct* were almost mandatory in terms of mending dolls and preparing jellies and desserts.

Homemaking of today, according to Mrs. Jackson, is primarily a purchasing, coordinating, and janitorial function. Specialists have taken over many of the homemaker's former functions, thus depriving her of the prestige and status stemming from exercising a definable skill. (One might argue that a generalist such as an executive has more prestige than a specialist. This is true in a large industrial organization, but a small family unit is not corporate enterprise.) Interior decorating consultants design draperies, sex education specialists preempt her expertise in this area, and food processors prepare some specialty dishes more economically and efficiently than can the homemaker.

Limited Rewards

Frustrations expressed by women about their lives repeatedly result from not being properly rewarded for their efforts. Few occupations in our society have such an unsystematic approach to rewarding good performance as does the homemaker role. Recognition, salary increases, promotion, transfer, letters of commendation, and additional benefits are examples of the kinds of rewards available in organizational life for those who perform at or above standard. Negative rewards also are not systematically dispensed to homemakers. Housewives are rarely fired for poor performance. Extreme acts of irresponsibility or disloyalty are usually required before a man will voluntarily incur the expenses involved in divorce. Even the basic reward of admiring the results of one's efforts are short-lived experiences for the homemaker. Attractively prepared meals are quickly eaten. Beds that are made become unmade; washed and ironed clothing becomes dirty and wrinkled within a pitifully short time span. Some housewives feel the mere complexity of their role is misunderstood and therefore unrewarded by men. One twenty-eight-year-old woman describes the situation this way: "Help! If only men knew what it was like to be a cook, nurse, economist, lover and a lot of other things and never have the time to become an expert at any one of them, then maybe they would know how hard this job really is. I don't think we housewives get enough credit."[15]

The single most consistent finding from our research with six hundred women is that they want more verbal praise from their husbands. Perhaps fifty women commented that their husbands were prompt in bringing poor performance to their attention (e.g. "Why is the house messed up?") but good or superior performance goes unnoticed. Housewives are not unique in this respect. Subordinates frequently lament that their superiors manage by exception—notice is made of performance below expectations while performance at or above expectation receives no comment.

Benjamin Spock wrote that ". . . few jobs outside the home—for women or men—are nearly as creative as that of raising fine children." Accepting Dr. Spock's observation as true, one might argue that homemaking thus becomes an inherently rewarding role that requires no external rewards such as verbal praise from husbands. Two fallacies are contained in this inference. First, child rearing is rewarding but the rewards are a long time in coming. Many years of observation are required before the success of a given child-rearing effort is known—often not until the child reaches adulthood. Second, child rearing is only one part of the homemaker's complex role.

Insipid Miscellaneous Demands

Homemakers, particularly in suburban areas, are pressured to engage in a multitude of activities peripheral to their central role. Activities such as attending PTA meetings, participating in community groups with no apparent goals, chauffeuring children and commuter husbands, and joining novice bridge groups are stultifying experiences to some women. These same activities, in contrast, can be major sources of life satisfaction for other women, depending upon their interests and *how* the activities are conducted.

The worst and most self-defeating motive for entering a group activity is to use that activity to fill the void in time created by mechanization of the homemaking task. Baking bread or washing clothes with a scrubbing board is a more psychologically rewarding experience for many women than attending a group meeting devoted to floral arranging. In contrast, if the motive underlying attending that same meeting were to learn more about floral arranging or to meet people, the experience might be more worthwhile. Activities without purpose are poor for one's mental health.

Social pressures are exerted upon men and women, particularly in smaller towns, to attend a variety of community activities. Many members attending these meetings lack clear definition of why the organization exists or why they are attending its meetings. Participating in a committee with no purpose is a lonely and sometimes humiliating experience. Again, if the committee members would confront their motivation for having come together the result might be more beneficial. The usual platitude is as follows: "This committee has been formed by responsible citizens who are truly concerned about the moral decay of our high school population." The more constructive (and honest) approach might be, "This committee has been formed because we are all a little bit bored and lonely as housewives. We pick on high school students because we are jealous of their ability to freely engage in fun. What can we do about our loneliness and despair?"

Negotiating with repair and service personnel about the maintenance of modern conveniences is another source of frustration that conceivably contributes the housewife syndrome. Automobiles, washing machines, and color televisions periodically malfunction, despite the magnitude of the initial purchase price. Many husbands have artfully delegated the tasks of coping with mechanical disasters to their wives. An alarmingly high proportion of repairs are either done improperly or not completed on time. This forces the homemaker to devote even more time to the unpleasant assignments of getting machinery repaired or confronting tradesmen about their mistakes.

The Housewife Syndrome Can Be Overcome

Pessimism has pervaded these pages so far. The housewife syndrome has been described as if it were an ominous malady permanently ingrained into the middle class woman's life style. Can the housewife syndrome be overcome? Is it changeable or correctable? Two opposite approaches to providing relief for this syndrome are well known—the revolutionary approach of some liberationists, and the suppressive approach of the traditionally minded. Our book attempts to provide a realistic and logical middle ground between these two extremes. Workable and feasible solutions to the problems of women are already available. More solutions will be available in the future.

Women's liberationists feel they have found the divining rod for overcoming the frustrations of housewives. The more radical feminists talk about revolution, confrontation, and overthrow of male supremacy with evangelical fervor. In their enthusiasm they neglect the important finding that most women, even dissatisfied housewives, seek approaches to more enriched lives which do not require an overthrow of present institutions. Chapter 2 examines in some depth both the legitimate, constructive demands of liberationists and also the limitations of this movement for many women.

Equally unsatisfactory as an antidote to the housewife syndrome is an attempt to gloss over, deny, or poke fun at the dilemma of the middle class housewife. Exhortations such as "Homemaking is the most wonderful, creative, complex, demanding, and self-fulfilling profession ever created by society" only add salt to the wound of the discontent. Intelligent, perceptive women recognize the denial of reality inherent in this kind of statement.

This book is optimistic despite its pessimistic beginning. We will examine in depth alternatives and options women have available to them. It is precisely through the exercising of these options that the transition from frustration and discontentment to satisfaction and contentment can be approached. Total contentment, adjustment, or euphoria is not the false promise we hold out. Some degree of discontentment and dissatisfaction goads people on toward a further exploration of the world around them. Discontentment in small doses is thus a constructive force.

Chapter 3, "Problems Created by Successful Husbands," is designed to provide you with insight into a psychological problem experienced by many women married to men of accomplishment. Similar to the housewife syndrome, this predicament appears correctable. Following this analysis of male-female problems created by success of the husband are four consecutive chapters geared toward overcoming some of the problems of women.

"Strengthening Your Self-Image," our Chapter 4, takes you on a step-by-step description of how one begins to establish self-confidence and design a plan for self-fulfillment. This counseling approach for normal people has been successfully applied to thousands of students and businessmen, but its application to housewives has just begun. This is our most important chapter for purposes of personal development.

Chapter 5 looks at realistic ways to improve the actual job of the homemaker. Industrial psychologists and other management advisors have improved the job satisfaction and productivity of a variety of people at work. These insights can also be applied to homemakers. Homemaking has *some* rewarding elements. Chapter 6, "Venture into the World, Outside," looks at some of the realities involved in finding fulfillment in a multiple role: that of homemaker and student, or homemaker and career woman. Husbands, it will be emphasized, must also undergo a slight change in role if their wives are to obtain a satisfactory transition.

Many women gravitate toward extramarital affairs as an antidote for the housewife syndrome. Every woman must reach her own conclusion about this solution. Chapter 7, "The Affair as a Solution," offers a close look at some psychological issues involved.

Women in search of a way out of their frustrations may want to become acquainted with the world as seen by their contented counterparts. Chapter 8, "Contented Homemakers," provides this opportunity. Many women experiencing discontent with their role have asked, "Am I normal?" Chapter 9, "Discontent or Disturbed?" provides some information to help you appreciate the difference between normal discontentment and emotional illness.

Some women may never overcome the housewife syndrome until men and other women are willing to cast aside outmoded stereotypes about the proper place of women in society. Chapter 10, "A New Taxonomy for Females," suggests a new approach to classifying women and illustrates that women can be both feminine *and* successful in the world outside.

Our final chapter, "Toward Self-Liberation," places what we have said on a philosophical level. In addition, twenty practical suggestions for personal growth are provided. Society may change its laws about women's rights, men may revitalize their perception of women, but the final responsibility for personal growth and change rests with the woman herself. This is the ultimate antidote to the housewife syndrome. Psychology can show you the path toward transition, society can open doors for you, but only you can make the transition.

NOTES

1. Norma Gorbaty is a fictitious name for a real person. All names given to people in case histories throughout this book are fictitious. Names of authors, of course, are properly identified.
2. Morton M. Hunt, *Her Infinite Variety: The American Woman as Lover, Mate, and Rival*, New York, Harper & Row, 1962, p. 5.
3. Betty Friedan, *The Feminine Mystique*, New York, Dell, 1970, p. 16. (Originally published by Norton, 1963.)
4. H. Gray, "The Trapped Housewife," *Marriage and Family Living*, 1962, pp. 179-182.

5. Review of Anne Richardson, *Up the Sandbox*, New York, Simon & Schuster, 1971, in *Time*, Jan. 25, 1971, p. 74.
6. P. H. Taylor, "Role and Role Conflicts in a Group of Middle-Class Wives and Mothers," *Sociological Review*, 12:318, Nov. 1964.
7. Annabelle Bender Motz, "The Roles of Married Women in Science," *Marriage and Family Living*, 23:374-376, Nov. 1961.
8. Chong Soo Pyun, "Monetary Value of a Housewife: An Economic Analysis for Use in Litigation," *American Journal of Economics*, 28:271-284, July 1969.
9. Edwin C. Lewis, *Developing Woman's Potential*, Ames, Iowa State University Press, 1968, p.
10. *Ibid.*, p. 90.
11. Clifford Kirkpatrick, *The Family*, New York, Ronald Press, 1963.
12. Philip E. Slater, "Must Marriage Cheat Today's Young Women?" *Redbook*, Feb. 1971.
13. Betty Friedan, *op. cit.*
14. Priscilla Jackson, Oakland University, personal communication.
15. Ronald Kistner, a former student of mine, gathered this quotation.

Chapter 2

THE WOMEN'S LIBERATION MOVEMENT

*Woman is the female of the species,
and not a different kind of animal.*

G.B. Shaw *Preface to Saint Joan*

Discontent with the homemaker role motivates many women to seek a transition into a new life style. The best publicized and most revolutionary approach to transition is the women's liberation movement. Women's liberation is a social movement attempting to move women toward economic, political, psychological, and at times even biological equality with men. Approximate synonyms include the "female rebellion," the "new feminism," and the "women's rights movement." The breadth, scope, and amorphous quality of this movement are reflected in the following definition prepared by a newspaper writer: "The movement itself might loosely be described as the aggregate force exerted by an unknown number of groups of two or more women who firmly believe that they are discriminated against solely because they are female."[4]

Rich historical precedent underlies this present-day revolt of a small minority of the majority sex (51 percent of people in the United States are female). Over fifty years ago American women won the right to vote via the Nineteenth Amendment. This milestone legislation passed in 1920 had its origins in a Women's Rights Convention in Seneca Falls, New York, in 1848. Three ideologically related events occurred in the 1960's to provide a forward thrust to the women's liberation movement.

First, *The Feminine Mystique*, published in 1963, provided a knowledge base for women's new discontent. Betty Friedan provided the American woman with a call to arms to overcome the shackles placed around her by a male-dominated society. Women were reminded that homemaking thwarts one's psychological growth, particularly the quest for self-fulfillment. The "feminine mystique" is essentially the role women are supposed to play in our society—one of passivity, docility, and contentment with homemaking as a full-time occupation. Betty Friedan indicts a male-dominated society (particularly marketing executives) for keeping women at home in order that they become better *consumers*. Over one and one half million copies of *The Feminine Mystique* have been sold, attesting to the relevance of its topic despite some lack of objectivity contained in the manuscript.

Mrs. Friedan's writing brought attention to an important social problem: the one she terms "the problem that has no name." This nameless problem is the dominant frustration in the housewife's role for many women. Being a homemaker–child-rearer–wife does not provide a broad enough range of psychological satisfaction for all women. Chapter 1, "The Housewife Syndrome," you will recall, examined this problem in depth.

Second, also during 1963, President Kennedy established the Commission on the Status of Women. This commission further alerted the public to the needs and problems of women. Recommendations generated by the Commission have led to the inclusion of prohibitions against sex discrimination in Title VII of the Civil Rights Act. The latter requires that all employees be treated without regard to sex in every phase of employment.[2]

The third event of the past decade lending strength to the women's liberation movement was the civil rights movement of the middle 1960's. If blacks were able to gain advantage by publicly making their views known, it was reasoned that perhaps women could achieve the same ends using similar means.

The civil rights movement also fostered the women's liberation movement in a paradoxical manner. The male-dominated character of the civil rights movement convinced a handful of women that there was injustice toward females even among revolutionaries. Role expectations dictated that "chicks" in the "New Left" were to cook, type, operate mimeograph machines, clean, and provide sex to male activists. This observation reinforced the notion that the times demanded a female liberation movement.

Male black leaders, as reported by Morton Hunt, also displayed some male chauvinistic attitudes of their own. One such leader commented, "The only position for a woman in SNCC is prone." Another leader of the New Left, when hearing of female discontent among members of the movement lucidly paraphrased Marie Antoinette with the following statement: "Let 'em eat cock."[3]

Women's liberation is not comparable to the black civil rights movement in two important ways. Blacks and whites, aside from skin pigmentation, are biologically and anatomically equal. Males and females are biologically and anatomically different, despite any protests from feminist thinkers to the contrary. Secondly, black extremists emphasize differences—black is beautiful. According to the credo of the feminist, to be female and feminine is not beautiful—to be a person on equal footing with men is to be beautiful.

Women's liberation from an organization-structure viewpoint is a wide collection of groups functioning autonomously. There is much less formal structure to the women's liberation movement than there is to groups such as the Boy Scouts of America or the Chamber of Commerce. The National Organization of Women (NOW) represents the largest, best-organized and perhaps the most moderate of the liberation groups. Founded by Betty Friedan in 1966, NOW claims a membership of about three thousand members dispersed among thirty-five chapters throughout the United States. One hundred of the members are male. NOW's primary goal is to end economic and legal discrimination against women, a goal shared by many men and women both within and without the women's liberation movement. Vehicles for change used by NOW include lawsuits and lobbies. Radical groups consider NOW to be the NAACP or "Uncle Tom" of the women's rights movement. According to Mrs. Friedan, one specific impetus to NOW *was* that many people told her women needed an organization such as the NAACP.

There is a basic ideological split between NOW and the more radical, militant women's liberation groups. NOW seeks to bring women into positions of power within society; the radicals demand changes in society. Radical feminists attract more attention in the popular media than do their more conservative counterparts. Maneuvers of the former have included brassiere burning in public view, demonstrations of cutting of tresses, and the disruption of Miss America contests. They are also the women who chant en masse:

Out of the houses,
Out of the jails,
Out from under!
Women unite![4]

Radical groups include Society for Cutting Up Men (SCUM), Women's International Conspiracy from Hell (WITCH), and Cell 16. SCUM is considered to be the most extreme of the liberation groups as reflected in their shibboleth that ". . . the male is a biological accident . . . an incomplete female, a walking abortion . . . To be male is to be deficient, emotionally limited; maleness is a deficiency disease and males are emotionally crippled."[5] SCUM members hope to bring about a complete female take-over of society and create a ". . . swinging groovy, out-of-sight female world."

The WITCH manifesto credits witches with being the first group opposed to female oppression. "Witches have always been women who dared to be groovy, courageous, aggressive, intelligent, nonconformist, sexually liberated, revolutionary."[6]

Boston's Female Liberation Movement (formerly Cell 16) is a radical feminist group that has achieved considerable media coverage, perhaps because its leaders include Abby Rockefeller, daughter of bank executive David Rockefeller. Complaints are voiced against conventional male sex techniques as fostering frigidity in women. They demand that women no longer use the last names of their husbands or fathers. *No More Fun and Games*, the Female Liberation Movement journal, urges women to dress in ordinary clothes, wear short cropped hair, desert their husbands and children, and avoid pregnancy. FLM also endorses more conventional feminist demands, such as revamping of abortion laws.

Basic statements of organizational philosophy made by SCUM, WITCH, and FLM must be interpreted as strategic attempts by these groups to bring attention to themselves. Similar to most revolutionaries, they value highly shock and confrontation techniques.

Accurate estimates of the membership size of women's liberation groups are unavailable. Groups exist both within the United States and other countries. Underdeveloped countries and Soviet Russia have no room for women's liberation. Women in underdeveloped countries do not have the time to think about female liberation. Russian women are already liberated. They are urgently needed to contribute to the labor force at unskilled, skilled, and professional-level occupations. Older women, no longer able to work in conventional jobs, sweep the streets. The government provides day care centers.

Morton Hunt suggested in May 1970 (talking about the United States alone) that in addition to a few hundred extremists, there are from five to ten thousand women who belong to all sorts of feminist groups.[7] Other estimates have run as high as fifty thousand actual members. The impact of women's liberation cannot be counted only in terms of its direct membership. Perhaps millions of nonjoiners are moderate feminists who express their orientation toward female rights in their letters to Congressmen and editors, reading habits, job preferences, sexual practices, marriages and divorces, and buying habits.

Activities conducted at women's liberation meetings center around group discussion (or rap sessions) about the female role in present society. Consciousness raising—the establishment of a common understanding of the problems that women face in a male-dominated society—is the goal of these sessions. Small group meetings are held about once a week to discuss a broad range of topics including attitudes toward work, families, careers, and women's role in society. The increased self-awareness that can occur in such sessions is illustrated by these statements quoted from *Time*:

> I was desperate when I came to Women's Lib . . . I always thought there had to something wrong with me because I wasn't exclusively interested in a life of suburban luxury . . . The first night I came to a rap group I had this suddenly close feeling because I found out other people had the same feelings about gut issues that I did.[8] *

Topics at liberation meetings also include approaches to speeding passage of legislation needed for women's rights. One committee of a women's liberation group in Westchester, New York, for example, concentrates on tax reform to allow women to deduct child care expenses. Another group has provided grass roots support for a woman candidate for the New York State Assembly.

What Kind of a Person Is the Liberationist?

Scientific information about the characteristics of women's liberation movement members is unavailable. However, tentative descrip-

*Reprinted by permission from *Time, The Weekly Newsmagazine;* Copyright Time Inc., 1970.

tions of demographic and psychological characteristics of liberationists, based upon information contained in newspaper and magazine coverage of this movement, can be offered. Several demographic trends among these women are apparent. The movement has its biggest impact in the big cities. Boston, to cite one illustration, shows heavy women's lib penetration. Based upon research into the role rewards and frustrations of housewives conducted by this author and his students, it is doubtful that some rural women are even *aware* of this movement.

Women who join the movement tend to be in their twenties and thirties and are college educated. College students, for example, are often active members of women's liberation groups. Many feminists are married and have children. As would be expected, the most active women in the movement do not have children between two and ten. Discretionary time is required for participation in any movement and mothers of young children are ". . . too busy to be liberated."[9]

There are very few blacks within the women's liberation movement. The majority of black women are still searching for more adequate civil rights. Women's liberation demands deal with problems that are more relevant once basic civil rights have been achieved. Psychologically, the white *female* and black *male* have more in common with respect to desire for more equal status in society. Black females, once their spouses have achieved more equal status in a white-dominated society, may themselves become more interested in liberation.

Psychological characteristics of women liberationists may appear to reveal more about them than do their demographic characteristics. Role discontent, or role frustration, probably exists among most of these women. (Many feminists would proclaim they are not discontent but simply concerned about human rights, not just women's rights.) Dissatisfaction is the motivating force underlying their joining a protest group. Members of the extremist groups appear to have deep feelings of anger, resentment, and frustration underlying their public actions. From their viewpoint anger and resentment are justified because of the injustices a male-dominated society has served them. More specific personality characteristics of liberationists include traits such as aggressiveness, and needs for autonomy and independence. Their intelligence level, as reflected by their higher than average formal education, is probably above average to superior.

Questions about the femininity of female liberationists frequently arise in conversations about them. Both males and females conditioned by traditional conceptions of male-female relationships (and these heavily influenced by Freud's psychoanalytic doctrine) perceive these women as having distinct lesbian tendencies. As expressed by a young Chicago secretary, "My husband assumes the militant women he sees on television are lesbians, that they don't have a man to occupy their life so they find other activities, like crusading, to fill their lives."[10]

Terms such as "man-haters," "castrating females," and "phallic-aggressives" are used by some critics to characterize the female liberationists. At worst these characterizations of liberationists are defensive maneuvers by traditionalists who want to preserve the status quo in male-female roles in our society. At best interpretations of the sexual orientation of feminists are overgeneralizations based upon accurate observations of a few of its members. One feminist leader announced in a press conference that she was bisexual, adding fuel to the lesbian argument.

The research upon which much of this book is based, and media coverage provide more accurate information about who the female liberationist is *not* than who she is. Traditional middle class housewives are anti–women's-liberation-movement, although they are in favor of equal rights for women. Four housewives in the fifty- to fifty-five-year-old age range, all of whom were married to blue-collar workers, provided identical reactions to the women's liberation movement: "They're crazy!"

Housewives of moderate education and limited occupational skills are psychologically threatened by the feminists. These housewives see the feminist movement as potentially forcing them to leave their homes and their husbands to enter an outside world in which they have little interest and for which they are ill prepared. In short, the antifeminists can be stereotyped as the church-attending, homemaking-oriented, small-town, moderately educated, white middle class female. Many black women, as explained earlier, and probably many upper class women also, fail to identify with the liberationists. Upper class women, it could be argued do not *need* the new feminism. Later in this chapter we will explore further why the female liberation movement is not for everyone.

What Do the Liberationists Want?

Demands of the new feminist groups are diverse, general, and specific. Different groups, depending upon their degree of radicalism or conservatism, propose different reforms. In broadest terms this movement, as articulated by NOW, wants to mobilize the conscience of society to recognize that the *rights of man* mean the rights of all men and all *women* equally. Following is an overview of what liberationists are demanding.

Equal Employment Opportunities

There is abundant statistical and anecdotal data available that women do not fare as well as men in the job market. *Harvard Business Review* reported a comprehensive survey of the attitudes of one thousand male and nine hundred female executives toward the role of women in managerial positions.[11] One major finding was that women have moderate but not equal opportunity in business. It is the rare, exceptional, *overqualified* woman who is able to succeed in management. Women in the United States occupy proportionately fewer professional positions than they do in other countries. Male-female imbalance in the physician population is frequently cited as lack of equal opportunity for women. Seven percent of physicians in the United States are female. Russia's physician population is 72 percent female. Only three countries reporting out of twenty-nine in one survey show a smaller proportion of female physicians than in the United States—South Viet Nam, Madagascar, and Spain.[12] Employment discrimination against women is also reflected in data such as the following:

> . . . the median earnings of women working full time are 58 percent of the corresponding figure for men. In 1968 the median income for fully employed men was $7,764. For women it was $4,457. Less than three percent of the women who work full time earn $10,000 or more; and in 1968 women held only 3.7 percent of government jobs that pay $14,000 and over.
>
> There are no women members of the Cabinet. There are only 12 women judges at the federal level. There are three women ambassadors. There are ten women in the House of Representatives and only one in the Senate. In 1967 women held 318 out of the 7,608 seats in the state legislatures, although there are more women voters than men.[13]

Even more central to feminist discontent are situations where males and females receive unequal pay for identical work. Male chemists with Ph.D. degrees earned an average of $15,600 in 1968. For women Ph.D. chemists the average earnings were $11,500.

Universities and colleges have also been known to give preferential treatment to males over females in their hiring and promotional practices. The proportion of women in academic positions has in fact declined from about 28 percent in the 1930's to 20 percent in the 1960's.[14] More significantly, the positions that women hold in academic institutions are different from the jobs held by men.[15] Women are more likely to teach undergraduates and to hold part-time positions than to teach graduate students or hold full-time positions. Women are much less likely to be employed by prestigious universities and much less frequently hold full professorships or key administrative positions.

Antifeminists might question the relevance of the information presented so far. Perhaps fewer women sought key positions because they attempted to maintain a dual career of mother and professor. Perhaps fewer women had time to devote to the professional activities necessary for advancement, such as publishing scientific and scholarly articles. L.S. Fidell conducted a unique *experiment* demonstrating that antifemale discrimination in hiring practices is found even in psychology departments.[16] (One would ordinarily think that psychologists, because of their basic concern for people, would be exempt from discriminating against any group.)

Specifically Fidell investigated the possibility that academic departments of psychology discriminate in hiring on the basis of sex. Brief descriptions of ten young Ph.D.'s in psychology were prepared and sent to the chairman of each of the 228 colleges and universities in the United States offering graduate degrees in psychology. Form A of the survey used feminine first names and proper pronouns for four of the hypothetical psychologists. Form B used feminine first names and proper pronouns for the *other four* hypothetical psychologists. The remaining two descriptions of psychologists were assigned male names to limit the number of female names on any one form. Here is one of the personal portraits used in the experiment:

> Dr. Alice (Albert) Baxter received her (his) degree in clinical psychology from the University of Washington. She (he) gets along well with her husband (his wife) but is not overly popular

with her (his) colleagues. Although she (he) appears serious about her (his) career as a researcher she (he) has published only two articles in the last five years, neither in prestigious journals.

Chairmen of the departments (or the persons in charge of hiring) were asked to make judgments about the psychologists based upon these brief histories. Judgments asked for included (a) current chance of his (or her) getting an offer for a full-time position, (b) the desirability of the candidate, and (c) what *level* of job: professor, associate professor, assistant professor, and so forth. At the end of the survey chairmen were asked to rank all the candidates from most to least desirable. Half of the chairmen received Form A, the other half Form B.

Clear sex differences were revealed by statistical analysis of the data. The level at which a Ph.D. psychologist would be offered a position depended not only on the person's academic credentials but also upon sex. Only men were offered full professorships. On the positive side from a feminist viewpoint, males and females were rated equally "desirable" by department chairmen.

Equal Rights Amendment

People of both sexes concerned about human rights have for many years attempted to push through passage of the Equal Rights Amendmend, which at this writing has passed through the House of Representatives. Originally drafted in 1923, this amendment provides: "Equality of rights under the law shall not be denied or abridged by the United States or any state on account of sex." Abiding by this amendment in both spirit and letter, according to some of its critics, will create both problems and opportunities for women. State laws prohibiting both sexes from using the same toilet facilities will be outlawed. Women could be required to pay alimony, lift heavy weights, and work more overtime. Proponents of the amendment feel this will provide full *psychological* equality for women. Women, under the provisions of this new amendment, will have identical legal privileges as men. Many old laws will become constitutionally suspect. Among them are the following:

> Laws that restrict the rights of married women to establish a legal domicile and, in some cases, engage in business; laws that exclude women from certain state colleges; laws that impose on them stiffer prison sentences; laws that govern the nation's arrangements as to

marriage, divorce, alimony and child support; and also, perhaps, laws that exclude women from the military draft.[17] *

Day Care Centers for Everyone

For women to fully exercise their options in society it is necessary for them to have easy access to the world outside the home. Children at home are a constraining influence. Adequate day care centers for children are recommended by feminists as the answer to this problem. Specifics of how such services will be financially supported are not included in the liberationists' demands. Presumably this could be a federal, state, or local government service. There is conflicting opinion about the effects of day care centers upon children.

Prestigious figures such as Margaret Mead have considered such day care centers as being harmful to children's psychological growth. Dr. Mead contends that too frequent changes of the mothering person place an emotional strain upon youngsters. "Children who are reared in institutions, while receiving perfectly adequate physical care, often sicken and die." The crucial factor in the child's development, according to Mead, is that someone must be available to give the small child continuing individual care and attention to help it grow into a mature adult. Day care centers, however, do not inevitably require that the mother surrogate change continuously. There is substantial evidence accumulated with the Israeli communes (kibbutzim) that children can prosper physically and emotionally under such a system.

Elizabeth E. Irvine, a child development specialist, conducted an extensive review of the empirical evidence as to the effects of the kibbutz on child development. Under this system each child receives two hours per day of undivided attention from the mother. The biological mother plays a crucial role in the first year of the child's life. Subsequently, the child is raised in a group setting under the supervision of a nurse-housemother. Irvine concluded that these children are *no worse*, and perhaps *better adjusted*, than those raised within their families. Later evidence has substantiated her findings. Disproportionate numbers of young men from kibbutzim are found in the most elite branches of the Israeli armed forces—the officers' corp and air force pilots.[18]

*Reprinted with permission of *The Wall Street Journal.*

Liberal Abortion Laws

Women's liberationists favor legislation in general that will facilitate female entry into the world outside the home. Unwanted pregnancies and their logical consequence—children requiring full-time care—are a deterrent to a career woman's life style. Liberalizing abortion laws would give women a choice about continuing an unwanted pregnancy. (Four states at this writing have such laws—New York, Alaska, Hawaii, and Washington.) This is the obvious reason that feminists demand more liberal abortion laws. Delving into more subtle, perhaps even subconscious concerns, it can be argued that more liberal abortion laws represent another way in which the female can assert her independence and make her own decisions. Employers invariably demand that women in advanced stages of pregnancy take a leave of absence. Pregnancy thus makes women temporarily dependent upon males (or in rare cases, other females) for financial support. Arrival of the infant furthers the dependency of the mother upon another person or institution for financial support. Readily available abortions allow women to make the final decision about terminating a pregnancy.

People are emotional about the subject of voluntary abortions. There are a host of religious and moral issues intertwined around this topic. Less controversial is the notion that a career-minded feminist (who sees children as interfering with her life style) would be a poor risk as a mother. Unwanted children have a low probability of being psychologically healthy children. Liberal abortion laws thus help prevent people from having children who have the potential to be psychologically damaging parents.

Overthrow of the Patriarchy

Radical feminists push for an overthrow of a patriarchial system in which (according to their perception) men control all of society's levers of power in government, industry, education, science, and the arts. Their specific aims and objectives in this area are diverse and far-reaching. Perhaps the most extreme and psychologically significant demand of the liberationists is for a revamping of standard English phrases which reinforce patriarchial values and attitudes toward women. As reported in *Time*, Varda Murrell has prepared a *Dictionary of Sexism*, denouncing the English language as "Manglish." She seriously advocates substituting "girlcott" for "boycott." Titles such as "Mrs." and "Miss," following the liberated approach, are replaced by the neutral "Ms." The zenith of absurdness is reached by the displacing of "history" with "herstory."[19]

Perception of women as sex objects is considered a patriarchial sin by both radical and more conservative feminists. Clothing stylists, television, and magazines such as *Playboy* are seen as villains in this regard. Gloria Steinem, a magnificently feminine feminist, offers the following *bons mots*:

> Playboy is partly responsible for Women's Lib. It supplanted brute strength as a symbol of maleness with sports cars and appliances. It made women objects more easily exchanged than sports cars, objects that become useless with age. There are times when a woman reading 'Playboy' feels a little like a Jew reading a Nazi manual.[20] *

The feminist viewpoint considers products geared to make women more feminine as being in reality products to make women more sexually attractive to men. Negligees, perfume, and cosmetics are seen as anathema to the cause. Cigarettes designed especially for women are subject to criticism by feminist groups. Fruit- and wine-flavored female personal hygiene products may have large appeal to many women, but the heated opposition they engender among feminists may lead to their decline. Even seemingly innocuous products such as household cleansers may be regarded as contraband by feminists because of the way in which they are advertised. Feminists unequivocally oppose portraying housewives as people of limited intelligence who are psychologically *turned on* by more effective products for discharging household tasks. Women's liberation groups have been particularly vocal in their condemnation of how television advertising portrays the female sex.

Antagonism toward such advertising has been the underlying force behind the creation of an organization called Media Women (and a newsletter on the subject), boycotts, and formal protests. Franchellie Cadwell, president of Cadwell Davis, Inc., has published a manifesto on television advertising which reads in part:

> When over 55 percent of women in the country are high school

*Gloria Steinem, from "What Playboy Doesn't Know About Women Could Fill a Book," *McCall's*, October, 1970.

graduates and 25 percent have attended college, when women have achieved sexual freedom, aren't they beyond 'house-i-tosis'? At the very least women deserve recognition as being in full possession of their faculties ... We know the rumbles have sounded. The revolution is ready and one of women's first targets will be moronic, insulting advertising ... No force has demeaned women more than advertising.[21]*

John Mack Carter, editor and publisher of *Ladies' Home Journal*, has already experienced the force that women's liberation might exert upon a business organization. Early in 1970, two hundred feminists marched into the *Ladies' Home Journal* office and made some pointed demands upon management. Their original demand was for Mr. Carter to turn management of his magazine over to an all-women staff selected by the movement. Carter was able to parry this demand by indicating that women were already a well-paid and respected majority of his staff.

Women's Liberation Is Not for Everyone

Women's liberation in the long range may directly or indirectly benefit all women. Equal employment and educational opportunities for members of both sexes perhaps will provide all women increased feelings of self-worth. For the short range—perhaps the next ten years—many women stand to be losers if the women's liberation movement were carried to its extremes. Many healthy, well-adjusted, basically satisfied homemakers and working women are unprepared by reason of skill or interest to be placed on an equal footing with men in society. Other women feel they are already given sufficient status in society.

Feminists argue that women who resist liberation are equivalent to the slaves who wished to remain with their masters after legislation had freed them. The elder slave was contented in his subservient role. In exchange for his diligence and obedience he received security and favorable working conditions. Younger and or more independent slaves might venture to the North and create new lives for themselves, but the older slaves lacked the psychological wherewithal to make the transition. The dependent, "faithful servant," older woman who perceives herself as being a loser in the liberation movement is illustrated

*Reprinted with permission from *TV Guide®* Magazine. Copyright © 1970 by Triangle Publications, Inc., Radnor, Pennsylvania.

by the following vignette, taken from *Ladies Home Companion*:

> Maud Thurston is in her fifties, neatly dressed . . . Her life re-
> volves around the president of a large corporation, Mr. Ross; he
> would be lost without Maud and she knows it...She has often been
> awakened by a telephone call in the early hours of the morning ask-
> ing her to look up some important facts for her boss... Maud has
> really very little private life of her own. She waits on Mr. Ross hand
> and foot, helps write his speeches, collects all the information he
> needs to impress his associates, and apart from her large salary, nev-
> er gets the credit for any of her work. Now the women's lib groups
> are screaming that secretaries are no better than slaves, just servants
> of their bosses, running into their offices at the sound of a buzzer,
> deferentially taking down on a shorthand pad their master's business
> letters, and later surreptitiously correcting the grammar and spelling
> so that he feels he really writes like Cash McCall... Maud is happy
> with her life; she feels she is needed and gets a vicarious thrill out of
> the powerful decisions he makes and the jet-set parties he attends...
>
> Maud's whole life has been based on service and devotion so that
> left to make a career for herself she would flounder completely with
> no strong male figure to actually make the final decisions and over-
> come opposition.[22]

Women who have not worked outside the home frequently have a
glamorized perception of the world of work. Those women who
have been forced to work out of *economic necessity* for lengthy
periods of time usually reject the notion of returning to work as
being a satisfactory life experience. Sociological research has clearly
indicated that women derive deep psychological satisfaction from
work when it is *their decision to work or not to work*. Surprisingly,
there are women who have worked at above average jobs who express appreciation for being allowed the privilege of fulfilling the
homemaker role. Annette Parker, a homemaker in a medium-size
community close to the Canadian border, expresses these sentiments:

> Those liberation girls have a lot of learning to do. They think
> working is all good and homemaking is all bad. I was a nursing su-
> pervisor for five years before we had enough money so I didn't have
> to work. This is a good life that I have now. I couldn't stand all that
> petty nonsense with the nurses and the doctors. Honestly, it was
> like having a headache everyday. The night hours were horrible
> and somebody was always complaining about something. Now I do
> what I want to do. I'm happy to let Jim (her husband) be the
> breadwinner in this family.

Early cultural conditioning has created a large class of women whose psychological needs are met by carrying out the contented homemaker role. (A later chapter is devoted exclusively to this phenomenon.) For these women, men are meant to be *numero uno*. Homemaking, child rearing, and receiving emotional and financial support from a stronger figure represent privileges to them. Parents take care of them when they are adults. Women who live by the credo of the feminine mystique are subconsciously terrified by some demands of the liberationists. Contented homemakers oppose passage of legislation which would facilitate divorces and make alimony settlements less female oriented. They hesitate *encouraging* husbands to leave them behind. Day care centers also are a threat to the women with the self-image of the homemaker; computers were similarly a threat to the bookkeeper. Sara McFarland, a woman I interviewed, cogently expresses the contented homemaker view of the feminists:

> *Question:* Sara, how do you feel about the women's liberation movement?
> *Answer:* Okay, maybe for somebody else it's good. Sure if I had big plans in life woman's liberation would help me. I don't have a book to write. I don't want to be an executive. Raising Robbie and Susie means one helluva lot more to me than any dumb job. Who needs it? I like my house, my children, and my husband is all right. Let those broads burn all the bras they want. I'll do what I want in life.

Maud Thurston, Annette Parker, and Sara McFarland reject the women's liberation movement for essentially similar reasons. They all thrive under a social system which makes females dependent upon males. Maud enjoys playing the "quiet helper behind the scenes" role in life. Annette has experienced the pressures of work outside the home at a responsible level, but opts to return to homemaker responsibilities. Sara is the contented homemaker stereotype. Another group of women reject the feminist movement for different reasons: those who have achieved the goals of female liberation without being feminists.

All Liberated Women Are Not Feminists
Earlier we mentioned that women's liberation is basically an educated, upper middle class, white phenomenon. Active participants in the feminist movement undoubtedly are discontent about their own

roles in life or sympathize strongly with the discontents of other women. Liberationists represent but a small proportion of well-educated, white, upper middle class women. Many upper middle class women, white or black, have achieved personal liberation without the aid of women's liberation. They have balanced career and family activities in an effective manner. Early in their marriages they were able to set meaningful goals and pursue them to the satisfaction of themselves and their families. These are exceptional women, but exceptional people provide good models for behavior. Comments by Helen Markel, chief articles editor at McCall's in 1970, illustrates the career woman-with-family whose sympathies do not lie with the liberationists:

> The last thing I want to do is alienate men. In fact, I think the ultimate test of maturity and pleasure in life is to make a strong and loving and lasting connection with one. Because I have always wanted to work, I have had to make certain sacrifices in my personal life and live with endless combinations of guilt and confusion and self-doubt about my relationship to my husband, my children, my job. (Do I really comfort, coddle, cajole, cope enough in any area to bring anything to anybody, or am I, in fact, a three way failure?) But I suppose one does what one has to do. Most of the women I know either work or wish they did, and in my more lucid moments I even believe that my husband and children are reasonably proud of me.[23] *

Still other intelligent, well-educated, and accomplished females do not share the discontents of the modern feminists and do not attend women's liberation meetings. Eli Ginzberg at Columbia University conducted a long-term follow-up study of the careers of three hundred mature women who had attended graduate programs at Columbia University in the 1945-1951 period. Approximately 40 percent of these women had pursued studies in the humanities, social sciences, or natural sciences. The remainder enrolled in the fields of education, social work, library science, journalism, business law, medicine, and public health. Ginzberg's major finding was that educated women, contrary to the prevailing popular belief, do not lead constricted and discontented lives. In contrast, they are in an advantageous position to pursue whatever goals they set for themselves. Most of these Columbia graduates were successfully married and

*Helen Markel, from *The Feminine Eye* by Shana Alexander, *McCall's*, July, 1970.

successfully employed in jobs that provided them personal satisfaction.[24]

How might a woman who is not super-educated, super-intelligent and super-motivated and who doesn't have a super-husband liberate herself without joining the women's liberation movement? *Women in Transition* is mostly about this very topic. Chapter 4, "Strengthening Your Self-Image," is a convenient starting point. One must first establish self-confidence, design a plan for self-improvement, and then begin putting the plan into action.

NOTES

1. *Times-Union*, Rochester, New York, May 23, 1970, p. 2D.
2. *Harvard Business Review*, July-Aug. 1965, p. 19.
3. Morton Hunt, "Up Against the Wall, Male Chauvinist Pig!" *Playboy*, May 1970.
4. Sophy Burnham, "Women's Lib: The Idea You Can't Ignore," *Redbook*, Sept. 1970, p. 188.
5. Julie Ellis, *Revolt of the Second Sex*, New York, *Lancer*, 1970, p. 65.
6. Julie Ellis, *op. cit.*, p. 57.
7. Morton Hunt, *op. cit.*
8. *Time*, Aug. 31, 1970, p. 19.
9. Sophy Burnham, *op. cit.*, p. 90.
10. *Wall Street Journal*, Aug. 4, 1970, p. 1.
11. *Harvard Business Review*, *op. cit.*
12. Janice Nupert Hedges, "Women Workers and Manpower Demands in the 1970's," *Monthly Labor Review* (U.S. Department of Labor), June 1970, pp. 19-29.
13. Sophy Burnham, *op. cit.*, p. 188.
14. L.S. Fidell, "Empirical Verification of Sex Discrimination in Hiring Practices in Psychology," *American Psychologist*, 1970, pp. 1094-1097.
15. A.S. Rossi, "Status of Women in Graduate Departments of Sociology: 1968-1969," *American Sociologist*, 5:1-12, 1970.
16. L.S. Fidell, *op. cit.*
17. *Wall Street Journal*, Aug. 10, 1970, p. 1.
18. *New York Times*, Dec. 31, 1970, p. 2.
19. *Time*, *op. cit.*
20. "What 'Playboy' Doesn't Know About Women Could Fill a Book," *McCall's*, Oct. 1970, p. 76.
21. Edith Efron, "Is Television Making a Mockery of the American Woman?" *TV Guide*, Aug. 8, 1970, p. 9.
22. Elizabeth Phillips, "The Losers in Women's Liberation," *Ladies' Home Companion*, Dec. 1970, pp. 1-10.
23. *McCall's*, July 1970, p. 8.
24. Eli Ginzberg, *Life Styles of Educated Women*, New York, Columbia University Press, 1966.

Chapter 3

PROBLEMS CREATED BY SUCCESSFUL HUSBANDS

*Being a husband is a whole-time job.
That is why so many husbands fail.
They cannot give their entire atten-
tion to it.*

ARNOLD BENNETT
The Title

Who Is a Successful Husband?

CINDY JORDAN, a former secretary of mine, is a divorcee with three young children. From her point of view, the wives of executives and professional men are people to be envied. Successful husbands, as she interprets the world, do wonderful things for their wives. These men provide their wives with luxuries such as fine clothing, their own automobiles, and suburban homes. Wives of successful husbands are not required to work outside the home and frequently even domestic help is provided. In times of divorce successful husbands can be relied upon to pay alimony and child support. Cindy's exaltation of the virtues of successful husbands is predictable from basic concepts about human motivation. People still concerned with managing such basic problems as providing physical necessities cannot look beyond these concerns and worry about more subtle psychological needs. Problems created by successful husbands relate to their wives' concerns about individual identity and emotional loneliness.

Before moving ahead with our discussion of their wives it is important to just briefly describe successful husbands. For the purposes of this discussion, *a successful husband is a married male who has achieved a high level of attainment in his primary occupational role (job). He derives considerable tangible and intangible reward from the process of reaching his career goals. He displays a relatively deep emotional and intellectual commitment to his work.*

Success cannot be measured in financial terms alone, but neither can money be neglected in arriving at a workable definition of success. To many people occupational success is roughly equated with a magnitude of earned income. Fortune magazine suggested in 1969 that the "good life" begins at $25,000 per year. Below this income level it is difficult to afford such luxuries as owning two late-model cars, sending children away to college, taking two vacations per year, and saving several thousand dollars annually. An annual income of $25,000 takes an average-size family outside of what I have labeled the "relief of discomfort zone."[1] Below this figure families still vascillate about making medium-sized purchases (e.g. "Can we afford a $100 cocktail dress?") and must carefully plan for larger discretionary purchases.

Although there are substantial differences in income opportunities in different fields (government, business, education, medicine, and so on) some people in every field earn in excess of $25,000 per year. College teaching, for example, is thought to be a low-paying field yet a large number of college professors have incomes that take them beyond the relief of discomfort zone. This is true particularly when all sources of income are added together—teaching, research grants, consulting, and writing.

Income levels required to achieve the good life, or take one outside the relief of discomfort zone, change every several years, because of a steadily increasing cost of living. To circumvent this problem of inflation, financial success can more accurately be defined as family income within the top 1 or 2 percent group. This conforms roughly to $25,000 per year in the late 1960's and early 1970's. Geography is also a significant factor. Living in the suburbs of major metropolitan centers always costs more than living in or near less-populated areas.

The subtle but psychologically significant point here is that success in the husband or father role is not implied by the term "successful husband." This chapter might be more appropriately called "Problems Created by Males Who Are Successful in Their Work and Also Happen to Be Husbands." The term "successful husband" reflects common usage and cannot be discarded because it requires elaboration and clarification.

With basic definitions out of the way, we can now examine two related characteristics of successful husbands that have a potential negative impact upon their wives' psychological well-being. These two characteristics have a significant impact upon and underlie the husband-derived dissatisfactions and discontentments of women. First, successful people in general, and successful husbands in particular, experience deep psychological commitment to their career. Boundaries between work and pleasure become blurred. To the successful vice president of marketing, sketching out ideas for the launching of a new product is ecstatic delight—not a chore imposed upon him by his company. Executive-level salesmen enjoy, relish, and actively search out opportunities to entertain clients in the evening. Entertaining customers is perhaps more psychologically rewarding to them than returning to the family situation at night. Successful executives in all fields lament that their days pass too quickly, not too slowly. Some successful men, partially because of their commitment to work, fall victim to the Sunday neurosis—feelings of psychological discomfort that occur almost exclusively on weekends. The Sunday neurotic experiences feelings of restlessness, tenseness, and discomfort when he is removed from his main source of psychological support, his work. Work for such people plays the important psychological function of *preventing* mental disorder.[2]

Second, successful husbands create problems for their wives because many of their highest-level needs cannot be met at home. Wives, children, and family life satisfy some but not *all* of a successful husband's psychological needs. Needs for love, companionship, affection, and sex are amply met by a healthy marital relationship. Wives also meet a complex of other needs a successful husband might have. Numerous executives have told me that an important role played by their wives is that of a confidential sounding board. Successful men are intense people and have an urge to intellectually unwind with a person they can trust. Wives often are frequently in a better position to effectively carry out this role than are colleagues or the executive's secretary. The successful career man is often unable or unwilling to take time during the day to free-associate with another person. Additionally, members of large organizations may feel it politically unwise to express their innermost fears and apprehensions to a boss, subordinate, or colleague. To do so may be interpreted as a sign of weakness—at least according to the perception of some successful men. The wife thus emerges as a vital confidante.

There are cravings for warmth, understanding, tenderness, and perhaps even mothering in even the most successful and hard-driving man. These desires are much better met through wife and child relationships than through work. (It would indeed be a rare competitive work situation that provided a man ample opportunities to be treated with understanding, tenderness, and warmth.) These functions can best be performed by women, children, and occasionally friends. The puritanical view is not being advanced here that wives to the exclusion of mistresses and girlfriends can perform these functions. The point stressed is that male-female and male-child relationships are the traditional mode by which such needs are gratified. My undocumented observation is that most successful men hardly have enough time to cope with their wives, much less look for long-term emotional gratification from a mistress.

What needs then cannot be met at home? The highest-level needs are labeled "egoistic" needs by behavioral scientists. Among these are drives or urges for tangible accomplishment, the acquisition of competence, and self-fulfillment—in short, drives for success. Successful men can rarely find outlet for such needs at home. (A central proposition in our book will be that women with strong higher-level needs also have to look beyond the immediate family environment for self-fulfillment.) The wife of a successful husband is capable of satisfying only a small segment of her husband's total range of psychological needs. Perhaps this hard psychological fact underlies the following statement from the wife of a highly successful man: ". . . I think the best husbands very often are failures in business because then a wife can be the most important thing to them . . ."[3]

Focusing upon one higher-level need will suffice to illustrate why it is extremely rare for a successful man's relationship with his wife and family to represent the dominant motivating force in his life. Self-actualization and achievement is considered by psychologists to be the apex of human needs. What a person can be, he must be. He is driven to pursue the limits of his potential. This need can be best satisfied by overcoming challenges, solving difficult and novel problems, and creating new institutions and objects.[4] These are characteristics found in most successful people. You might argue that a husband should be content with moderate success and then find creative outlets for his needs in hobbies such as woodworking and home repairs. The underlying flaw in this argument is that high-level accomplishment can best be measured by the standards of society. External rewards in the form of accolades and financial incentives are heaped upon the author of a best-selling book, or the company president, but none of these accrue to the man who builds his own patio. Men less imbued with drives for achievement can and do satisfy a broader range of needs at home.

The point we have developed should not be interpreted to mean successful husbands do not appreciate their wives or find home life stultifying. However charming, beautiful, compassionate, and clever a woman is, she cannot hope to become a substitute for meaningful work. Motivational theory even suggests that an adequate home situation is almost a precondition for wanting to overcome challenges in the world outside the home. Until needs for love and affection are relatively well satisfied, a man may not be as strongly motivated to pursue achievement, accomplishment, power, and status. His energies are still focused upon meeting these more basic needs. During a marital argument the wife of a successful husband exclaimed, "You don't care about me as a person. You have your work and I'm just a housekeeper and a sex partner to you."

From the man's point of view this was an oversimplification of his personal motivation. He certainly sees sexual relationships and his work as important, but also recognizes the complexities of human motivation. His retort illustrates the importance of satisfying needs for affection and understanding. "That goes to show you don't know what the hell you're talking about. When you're not pestering me at home, I can turn out much more work."

Having a home situation that adequately takes care of important concerns such as sex, love, affection, understanding, and emotional support is perceived by some men as the psychological equivalent of having money in the bank. Money stashed away provides a secure feeling, but only surface attention is paid to it except in times of crisis or particular need. The successful man thus neglects the very thing that is providing him an underlying feeling of security—his relationship with his wife or his financial resources.

Psychological Distance Hurts More Than Physical Distance

Successful men are busy people. Their work often keeps them away from home during dinner hours, overnight, and occasionally on weekends. It is not uncommon for successful businessmen to spend 40 percent of their nights away from home on business trips. Corporate executives of multiplant companies typically log over 100,000 air miles per year. University presidents find an evening at home with their families a luxury. One college president lamented that he rarely shares dinner at home with his family more than two nights per month. Wives of mobile husbands often comment about the uncanny ability of their spouses to be away from home at times of crisis with the children. Statements such as the following are not unusual:

> When Paul (the husband) was in Miami on a convention our youngest son fell over the front of his bike and had a concussion . . . Margie slipped in school and came out of it with a deep cut over her eye. Who remembers where Paul was then? I felt at that time, why even bother having a husband? . . . It's always me alone at the PTA. I overheard someone say that she thinks I'm really divorced.

The physical separation caused by the demands of work undoubtedly creates unwelcomed pressures on many wives and children. Parenthood and home management proceed more easily when the responsibility is shared between two full-time spouses. Problems created by physical separation, however can be much less devastating to women than the psychological distance that often exists when the husband is home. Many women adjust well to the frequent absence of their husband during weekday nights. Some women capitalize on this opportunity to pursue their own interests and hobbies. Another workable solution is for women to join forces with the children in having less formal and more relaxed evenings. One example here is the hamburger supper served on cardboard plates in place of a more formal family dinner.

Psychological distance when the husband is home hurts more than the problems created by physical separation stemming from work schedules. The following anecdote illustrates how attention focused on work can be perceived by the spouse as psychological distance.

> Dr. Elliot Burns, a physician and hospital administrator, has a meeting the next day with the hospital board of trustees in order to

seek approval for physical expansion of the hospital. Cynthia, his wife, has just learned that Wendy, their youngest daughter, has slipped from the middle to the bottom reading group in the fourth grade. Cynthia initiates conversation about the reading problem and spends five minutes presenting all the details as relayed to her by the teacher and Wendy. Arthur responds, "Yeah, that is interesting."

Cynthia interprets his response as symptomatic of Arthur's preoccupation with work and consequent neglect of important family matters. Arthur interprets this conversation from a different point of view. His perception is "How can she bother me with Wendy's fourth-grade reading when I'm facing an eleven-million-dollar decision tomorrow?"

Physical distance can in some instances foster psychological closeness because the couple makes better use of time when they are together. Additionally, not all successful husbands are preoccupied with their work. There are rare people who can tune out career thoughts when at home. A vice president of planning I know represents the rare individual who can overcome the problems of physical distance and work preoccupation when he is home. This man works for a company with multiple locations which dictates that he spend three to four nights away from home per week. He talks so glowingly about his marital relationship that I was prompted to ask him how his marriage withstood the rigors of his job. His analysis perhaps points the way toward overcoming the problems of physical and psychological distance.

When I'm home, I'm really home. It's like a honeymoon when I come home on Thursday night. I never think about work when I'm with my wife. Because of my heavy travel, we never seem to get tired of each other. I appreciate my wife more since I've taken this job and I think she gets a bigger bang out of having me around the house when I am home . . .

Successful people often reach their levels of accomplishment because of a deep commitment to their work which can have negative consequences for their marriage. This commitment often manifests itself in preoccupation with business even when physically removed from the place of work. One successful life insurance salesman makes the following comment: "Even when I am home at night, I'm planning the next deal. If I'm working on a $100,000 whole-life policy, I can hardly pay much attention to my wife's complaint that the washing machine is making a terrible noise."

Wives of successful men have noted that their husbands' preoccupation with work transcends waking hours. One public relations executive said it annoyed his wife that he talked about clients in his sleep.

Part of my standard procedure in attempting to understand the needs for growth of a manager is to ask him to tell me about his faults as perceived by his wife. Managers at higher levels in organizations show a remarkable consistency in their response to this question. Wives perceive these men as being poor communicators more than any other single criticism. Further questioning and analysis suggests that this poor communication relates more to listening than to talking. Executives involved in their work may find no difficulty in *sending* messages to their wives. Communications problems arise in the *receiving* of messages. Social psychologists have accumulated ample evidence that effective communication is a *transactional* process—both parties must participate in the communication process. Impoverished listening is interpreted by the wife as a lack of interest in her as a person on the part of the husband. Feelings of lowered self-esteem often result from the perception that one is not valued as a person. The wife placed in such a psychological bind often retaliates with direct verbal aggression toward her husband. Frequently the aggression is redirected toward his career and his success. Aggression directed toward the husband and his career manifests itself in the form of *resentment*.

Successful Husbands Are Sometimes Resented

Resentment appears to be the emotion underlying the frustrations and dissatisfactions of most wives of successful husbands. Such resentment may have multiple roots and, as alluded to above, may be expressed directly at the husband or indirectly toward his work, career, boss, or organization. Resentment, it must be carefully emphasized, is not necessarily an irrational or unhealthy emotion. It can have logical justification. The following episode between a husband and wife illustrates the latter's resentment directed toward the husband's work.

Ralph Carter is an economist employed as a faculty member of a midwestern university. He has worked three nights a week for four months preparing a research article for submission to *Harvard Business Review,* perhaps the most prestigious magazine within his field. Placement of his article in this magazine carries considerable weight in terms of receiving acceptance from his peers. Furthermore, publication in this journal could accelerate his career progress. Carter's article was accepted providing he make some changes which he assumed would require only three more nights of work. Upon arrival at home one night, Carter told his wife Carolyn the significant news. He apologized for having to cancel their agreed-upon evening out together that night. He suggested that once the article was completed there would be time for amusement and recreation. Carolyn replied, "Take that miserable, goddamn article, rip it up and dedicate it to our marriage. If you don't, we're through."

Ralph Carter spoke, "*Harvard Business Review* means a helluva lot more to me than you do. A man can easily find another wife, but how often can you get an article published there?"

One might argue that this husband-wife interchange is an example of open communications, and therefore healthy. However, it also illustrates the reciprocity that occurs when resentment or hostility is directed toward another person. Resentment evokes counter-resentment. Counter-resentment adds fuel to the resentment cycle. Feelings and attitudes become exaggerated in intensity. Professor and Mrs. Carter's exchange also points to a central factor underlying many situations of women resenting their husbands. The *attention* successful men pay to their work is resented by many of their wives. As oft mentioned here, deep emotional commitment to work characterizes successful people. This careful attention successful husbands pay to their work is often perceived by a wife as exceeding the attention she receives as an individual. Comments by Dr. Robert C. Sorenson, a sociologist, in his analysis of questionnaires completed by the wives of successful men, cogently explain this form of resentment: "Some women consider business his mistress. . . . Is unfaithfulness the person or the thing with which a man is involved?"[5]

Intertwined with feelings of resentment toward successful husbands are feelings of competitiveness. Competition exists in a subtle and indirect manner. There is obviously not direct competition between the successful husband and his wife over matters such as earning money or doing the best job on particular household chores. Even the woman with a career of her own has characteristically begun her career too late in life to seriously compete with the husband over earning levels or occupying a bigger job in an organization. Rarely would couples in anything approaching a normal marital situation compete over household tasks. Competition over the affection of children should be no more frequent in the homes of successful husbands than in other homes.

What form of competition is then likely to exist? Wives of successful husbands often consciously or preconsciously feel competitive about occupying *numero uno* position within the family. Friends, relatives, and perhaps children often perceive the successful husband as being the more significant member of the marital team. "I don't want to be your shadow," said the wife of a Congressman. Popular terms used to identify married women undoubtedly engender some form of resentment and incite feelings of competitiveness. Many women feel uncomfortable being the "distaff" side of somebody else. (A distaff is really the staff for holding the flax or wool in spinning, thus less than a position of superiority or equality however necessary its function.) However democratically a family unit is organized, it is difficult for the wife of a successful husband not to be perceived as occupying the number two role within the family. The feeling of being number two often triggers these feelings of competitiveness toward the person occupying the number one position.

Resentment toward the successful husband stems also from the comparison some women make between their role and that of the husband. Successful husbands are often seen as leading a dynamic, rewarding existence characterized by contacts with a wide variety of interesting people. Their day and many of their evenings involve contacts with mature, responsible *adults*. In short, many wives of successful men feel that their husbands have a more interesting role than that of a housewife. Should you need statistical evidence to support this point, an earlier *Fortune* magazine survey indicated that 50 percent of women had this perception. Many husbands have come to recognize one social amenity that should be used sparingly with mothers of preschool children. Asking "What's new?" upon arrival at home can trigger resentment on the woman's part. This is particularly true to the extent that the wife perceives her role as stultifying and her husband's as glamorous and dynamic.

Successful men usually have jobs they perceive as interesting and dynamic. Not all men are successful and not all men have exciting jobs. Many men in professional-level occupations such as accounting and engineering may be involved in daily activities they interpret as psychologically unrewarding and static. Their work schedule is structured for them by external factors. One husband in group discussion about housewives mentioned that he envied his wife's freedom to manage her own time and the diversity in her life. He interpreted luncheons, bridge clubs, and reading during the day as representing more diversity than was feasible in his life.

Observe that I am alluding to resentment episodes in which the less successful spouse feels resentment toward the more successful spouse. Agreed that in most cultures the male is typically the member of the marital team that has the better opportunity for achieving success. Several years ago I encountered an example of "role reversal" with respect to female-toward-male resentment. A male statistician was married to a female advertising executive. She was of similar age and educational level but her annual income was ten thousand dollars higher. Several hours elapsed in discussions with the statistician before he was willing to talk about his wife's success and how it affected their marriage. He attributed much of her accomplishment to "good breaks." This couple was married shortly after both graduated from college. They grew career-wise at unequal rates and her rapid progress and success provoked resentment on his part.

Conspicuous Consumption Resolves Only Some Problems

Conspicuous consumption to many people is a culturally expected and socially accepted way of meeting their needs for status. Wives of successful husbands are expected to be active consumers of goods and services that are more luxury items than necessities. This role expectation is more pronounced in key metropolitan areas such as New York and Los Angeles than in less-populated areas. Retail shopping, to many New York City women, is an activity of value within itself. The *process* of shopping is perceived as an exciting experience in its own right, outside of any particular *function* shopping performs. Buying an oil painting provides more psychic rewards than observing it once hung in the home. Shopping for a cocktail ring becomes as much a source of satisfaction as using the ring. Similarly the act of planning for and being able to afford an expensive vacation is as much a source of satisfaction as the actual process of participating in the vacation. Walking around the streets of India may be no more culturally enlightening than visiting the slums of Chicago, but the Indian trip has one distinct advantage. Other people full well recognize that a family trip to India is a grand act of consumption. Anybody living in Chicago can afford a trip to its slums but few can afford a trip to India. Only affluent people can afford to consume for the sake of consuming.

Conspicuous consumption runs the danger of becoming a shallow and unrewarding pursuit. Purchasing goods financially less successful people cannot afford represents less than an opportunity for self-fulfillment to many women. Active consumption of goods and services provides the largest psychological rewards before a woman passes the financial "relief of discomfort zone." Successful husbands, by the definition I provided earlier, have passed this income zone. Items such as annual vacations, memberships in country clubs, and the occasional purchase of an original painting cease to be major decision points in a marriage.

Rachel Forsythe, the wife of a partner in a law firm (income of $33,000 in 1970), succinctly expresses the limits to which the purchase of material objects can gratify her needs:

> Goddamnit, I have all the things I need. When the old car broke down, my husband bought a new one for me. Both children are in nursery school. As my husband says, I have spent more time trying on outfits in the ski shop than time on the slopes. This year he bought me the exact same bracelet he bought for me last Christmas. After buying me jewelry for eleven years, he's forgotten what I own or don't own. There are at least ten books on the shelf I've bought but not read. We're certainly not rich, but some of the clothing I throw out looks better than what some of my neighbors wear.
>
> Despite all these darn things, I'm not happy. I'm lonely and miserable. My husband thinks I'm an ingrate because despite my nice home and all the things we own, I complain a lot. I would trade all this junk tomorrow if I thought Gary would care more for me and less about his law practice . . .

Rachel Forsythe's feelings illustrate the limits to which conspicuous consumption can provide emotional satisfaction to the wives of successful husbands. There is good reason to believe that if Mrs. Forsythe were not in an economic position to drive her own car, ski, or send her children to nursery school, she would focus on money as a source of dissatisfaction. Paradoxically, once these luxuries are available they no longer are a source of concern. They have lost their potency as a motivating force for the wife of a successful husband. Once a desire for conspicuous consumption diminishes she intensifies her concern about having an adequate emotional relationship with her husband. This adequate emotional relationship often requires that the husband invest more psychological energy in his wife and less in his career. Many men successful in their careers, unfortunately, cannot simultaneously satisfy the psychological needs of their wives.

Conspicuous consumption, then, resolves only some problems of women. Earlier in marriage, the successful husband is valued for his ability to gratify his wife's status needs through the ability to acquire material goods and services. After several years of buying for the sake of buying, the rewards from conspicuous consumption diminish. Planning for the purchase of a large home and finally realizing the plan represents an important emotional experience for many couples. After several years of being financially successful, such matters are perceived as less important. Once this occurs, the successful husband may be resented for the very facet of his behavior for which he was cherished earlier. When ability to purchase goods was more valued by his wife, his commitment to work was a virtue. When consuming becomes less meaningful than emotional closeness and attention from the husband becomes more important than material goods, he runs the risk of being resented for commitment to his career.

Successful Husbands Are of Some Value

This chapter has focused upon problems created by successful husbands, but we cannot afford to lose perspective. Many women find considerable psychological reward in being married to a successful person. Being "Mrs. Success" (author Lois Wyse's term) represents an exciting and rewarding role to these women. One might argue that the chauffeur, maid, secretary, or bootblack of a successful man experiences the same psychological rewards. Anecdotal evidence and research results suggest that the situation is more complex. Being married to a successful husband gratifies a variety of needs and desires.

Auren Uris, a management writer of long-standing reputation, conducted a survey of how wives of printing industry executives felt about their husbands and their careers. (All were wives of presidents and vice presidents, thus fitting our criteria for being married to successful husbands.) The dominant finding of the study was that most of the executives' wives experienced a feeling of involvement in their husbands' careers and therefore did not resent their husbands' jobs.

> Among the 79 percent who answered No to the question, "Is your husband's job hard on you? not only were there statements such as, It's a part of our marriage, and we both accept it, but there were indications of actually enjoying the challenge.[6]

Another interpretation of the comments made by these women is that many find gratification in contributing to the executive's success. ". . . The wife apparently finds a sense of importance and meaning in life's scheme by providing the kind of support that makes it possible for the husband to meet the demands of his job."[7]

Women who find reward in enhancing their husband's career and sharing in his victories evidence some similarity in interests to teachers, coaches, and staff advisors. Teachers, to truly enjoy their role, must often be content to provide ideas to students who eventually become more successful than themselves. One business school professor I know has been instrumental in enhancing the personal wealth of many of his students. He finds meaning and reward in providing financial advice to others and derives no personal financial gain from these activities. Similarly, the football coach of an All American player receives less notoriety and recognition than the player. Psychic rewards come to the coach by vicariously sharing in the successes of his pupil. Staff advisors in large organizations feed information to their bosses to help the latter in decision making. The boss, in turn, capitalizes on these ideas and their origin is quickly forgotten. Staff advisors must find gratification in working quietly behind the scenes to assist their supervisors.

Wives of successful husbands receive a greater return on investment of time in their husbands than do the wives of less successful husbands. Women who have supported their husbands through medical school consciously or preconsciously perceive their high income and status later in life as some kind of retribution for their early struggle. Similarly, the woman who has worked as a waitress to subsidize a husband's efforts at writing a novel feels she has made a wise investment when the novel becomes a best seller. Expressed in simple economics, we can conclude that at least the wives of successful husbands get adequately compensated for helping their husbands along in their careers. The story is much different for most women.

Women play perhaps an even more supportive role in the career of unsuccessful husbands. I have been struck by the extent to which many men of modest accomplishment are provided emotional, financial, and intellectual support by their wives. Several times within the last year I have encountered wives of students who have typed, virtually written, and finally hand-delivered to the professors their husbands' term papers. Salesmen have told me how their wives help them plan appointments and on occasion even line up prospects for them. Once I recommended to a young middle-manager that he take steps to improve his report-writing skills. He replied, "I guess I should, but I usually use my wife for that. I tell her what I want to say and she puts it down on paper for me." Several students of mine have acknowledged that they are pursuing a master's degree in business administration because of their wives' insistence. Many men attend undergraduate programs for the same reasons. They are reacting to their wives' demands, not their own internal push.

Wives of successful husbands, I suspect, have to invest less emotional and physical energy into their husbands' careers. Several different interpretations can be made of this apparent social injustice. First, successful husbands probably require less external push. They are self-motivated men who would rise to their potential with or without the help of another person. Second, it is conceivable that a woman providing too much help to a man reinforces his tendencies toward lack of self-sufficiency. His immaturity and lack of direction is further ingrained by an understanding wife who prods him on toward his every success. (You might rebut that many men would gravitate toward career destruction without continual prodding by their wives. This is hard to refute without some carefully conducted psychological research.)

Marriage to a successful husband provides yet another important psychological reward. The woman who marries a successful man has fulfilled a criterion for female success that early cultural conditioning has established for her. Female success, according to this cultural stereotype, is importantly a function of marriage to a successful male. Fewer parents in the future will impose this cultural value upon their daughters. There are gradually changing expectations for women in our society. Traditional measures of female success are eroding away through the pressures of women's liberation and the attitudes of younger people. Female success is coming to be measured not solely in terms of the husband's accomplishment, but also in terms of the woman's own accomplishment.

Nevertheless, the notion that a woman is a successful person to the extent that she is married to a successful person remains a hardened cultural value. Women born in the 1920's cling tenaciously to the belief that their adequacy as parents can be measured by the accomplishment level of their daughters' husbands. To the extent that a daughter marries an affluent person and their marriage endures, the parental influence has been beneficial. Educational or occupational success of the daughter is a less important measure of parental success. The mother of three girls, each of whom married stable professional men, made a statement that vividly illustrates the cultural stereotype to which we allude: "Sure my daughters criticize me as a parent and kid me about the way I've raised them. It doesn't bother me. The proof is in the pudding. Look at the men they married."

Horse breeders are judged by the swiftness of the horses they raise. Women are judged, according to this cultural value, by the occupational success of their husbands.

Resolving the Conundrum

The basic tenet of this chapter is that successful husbands create a unique set of problems for their wives. Undeniably, being married to a man of moderate success, low success, or even failure presents a different constellation of problems. Coping with a husband's frustrations and failures may represent a bigger challenge than coping with her successes. Many middle class women complain that their husbands' primary commitment is to watching athletic events on television during the fall and winter. Some men are uninvolved in both their careers and their family. Perhaps this is a source of more intense frustration to women than any of the problems faced by the wives of successful husbands. Nevertheless, "Mrs. Success" faces her own set of problems.

Underlying many of these problems are feelings of jealousy, resentment, and envy toward the successful husband and his accomplishments. For the woman this situation becomes both a conundrum and a challenge. Many women regard it puzzling that wives of successful husbands have problems and frustrations. Challenge faces the wife of a successful man who wants to effectively deal with her feelings of resentment and competitiveness toward him. For now we will mention briefly *what* needs to be done. Chapter 4, "Strengthening Your Self-Image," will tackle this formidable task.

Eric Hoffer, longshoreman, labor leader, and modern philosopher, wrote in a newspaper column that ". . . a man who is doing something he thinks is worthwhile envies no other man." Similarly the woman who feels she is doing something worthwhile—independent of her husband's successes—is less likely to feel resentment and envy toward her spouse. The woman who establishes her own identity and uniqueness as an individual is no longer jealous of those people close to her (e.g. her husband) who have achieved this milestone in personal growth. In recognition of this curious phenomenon, successful husbands often welcome and encourage their wives to pursue interests that are fulfilling and rewarding. An advertising account executive made the following observations during a counseling session:

> My wife is more fun to live with since she became engrossed in selling mutual funds. She is away from the house a lot and I miss having her around, but it's worth it. She doesn't bug me anymore about being more interested in advertising than in her. For the first time in our marriage I can ask her about what she is doing and feel I won't get a smart answer. I notice she's more even-tempered toward the children now that she's into something heavy of her own.

Feelings of personal inadequacy may also underlie anger and resentment directed toward husbands who are psychologically involved in their occupational activities. Feelings of inadequacy, similar to feelings of jealousy, can best be overcome by a person developing a positive self-concept. Positive self-concepts do not come easily. To "feelgood about yourself," as contemporary language describes it, one must first accomplish something that you and others feel is valuable. For some women this might mean organizing a Christmas-time children's art show. For others it might entail having a magazine article published. There is no single achievement that will bolster the self-worth of all women.

In short, many of the problems created by successful husbands are feelings of resentment, jealousy, envy, and perhaps even inadequacy their behavior precipitates in their wives. Attempting to move your husband away from career involvement may prove to be more frustrating than attempting to develop your own uniqueness as an individual. Establishing yourself *sui generis* is perhaps an even more worthwhile and rewarding pursuit than attempting to direct your husband's intellectual energies away from something that is vital to his self-image. Our next chapter focuses upon the first steps toward revitalizing yourself as a person.

NOTES

1. Andrew J. DuBrin, *The Practice of Managerial Psychology*, Elmsford, New York, Pergamon Press, 1971.
2. Otto Fenichel, *The Psychoanalytic Theory of Neurosis*, New York, Norton, 1945, p. 472.
3. Lois Wyse, *Mrs. Success*, Cleveland, 1970, p. 15.
4. David R. Hampton, Charles E. Summer, and Ross A. Webber, *Organizational Behavior and the Practice of Management*, Glenview, Ill., Scott, Foresman & Company, 1968, p.
5. Reported in Lois Wyse, *op. cit.*, p. 89.
6. Auren Uris, "Your Business Is Her Business," *Nation's Business*, May 1970, p. 73.
7. *Ibid.*, p. 74.

Chapter 4

STRENGTHENING YOUR SELF-IMAGE

Know thyself.
THALES (Diogenes/Laertius)

Why Strengthen Your Self-Image?

THE PROBLEMS of women discussed so far have a negative impact upon the self-image. Long-term dissatisfaction with your life style or some of its key elements erodes away your self-confidence. Perpetual frustration and disappointment lead to feelings of defeatism. Defeat also lowers self-confidence. Lowered self-confidence in turn leads to a more negative or weakened self-image. The self-image must be strengthened to provide the basic chassis upon which an improved life style can be built. Many housewives remain in emotional ruts because they lack sufficient confidence to even attempt a solution to their problems. Before exotic or long-range solutions to problems can be realized, an initial first step in a positive direction must be taken. Courage is required for this vital first step.

Taking that first step is perhaps more important than *what* step is taken first in the quest for self-realization. Gerald Self, formerly the head psychologist at the Continuum Center for Women (a unit of Oakland University in Rochester, Michigan, organized to provide life planning assistance to women), made this observation:

> I don't think it matters so much what she does, it's the doing that's important. She mustn't substitute introspection for action. A lot of women engage in endless philosophic discussions of what is really right for them—which course of study, which type of job. They persuade themselves that they're doing something when they're really just *avoiding* action. The realistic woman is willing to take a chance on something that may not turn out to be exactly what she wants. No matter what happens, she'll learn from the ex-

60

perience; taking one step gives her the courage to take another.[1] *

Women who have endured in the housewife's role for a number of years develop inhibitions about their ability to *untrap* themselves. Constructive approaches to self-improvement and self-development are perceived by these women as activities for younger women who have recently attended school. These attitudes are self-defeating and represent major stumbling blocks to mapping out a workable plan for self-fulfillment. Negative self-images are reflected in the following rationalizations offered by housewives in defense of their remaining in psychological traps.

> Am I too old?
> Can I compete with younger women?
> Will I feel out of place on campus?
> Can I still learn?
> Have I the stamina to take on two jobs?
> What have I got to offer?
> How do I know what I want to do? I don't know much about the world outside.[2]

Underlying such statements is perhaps an understandable fear of failure. The woman unconsciously guards against possible embarrassment from the reactions of friends and family if she fails in her pursuit of self-development. One woman inquiring about an evening college course questioned if the institute would send a copy of her grades to her husband. This naivete is but a symptom of the unsureness that besets many women who embark upon a program of self-improvement.

Results stemming from attempts at self-improvement are never guaranteed and the process is time consuming. Careful planning, courage, and determination are required to make the transition from the frustration of higher-order needs to a satisfying level of self-realization. *Planning*, as applied to personal development, is a less formidable idea than it sounds. In practice it involves deciding upon a group of activities or experiences that will help you approach self-realization. "What steps do I have to take to receive a larger share of psychic rewards in life?" is the question planning attempts to answer. Before this map for a new life plan can be drawn, two real-izations must take place. First the woman must recognize that she has a problem and *desire* to change. Second, a substantial amount of self-knowledge is required. Insight into one's abilities, aptitudes, prefer-ences, and motivations is perhaps never complete, but partial insight is usually enough to begin the transition toward a more rewarding life style.

Self-Knowledge Is Crucial

Self-improvement begins with a careful analysis of your history, traits, characteristics, and preferences. Introspective people, by defi-nition, frequently examine their own thoughts, preferences, feelings, and motivations thus already possessing a modicum of self-knowl-edge. Introspection, however, often proceeds on a haphazard basis. Making the transition toward a higher level of self-realization or self-fulfillment requires a more systematic approach to acquiring knowledge about oneself. I have been struck by the exhilarated feel-ing many people experience at the moment of discovering something significant about themselves. Said a twenty-seven-year-old adminis-trative assistant, "You're right, now that I've looked at it, my biggest problem is that I take care of my husband is if he were a lazy child." *Insight* is the label given to this type of sudden realization.

Self-knowledge for the purposes of personal planning can be ac-quired by two readily available approaches. One approach, to be pre-sented first, requires that you do all the work without the assistance of a professional counselor. Formal counseling approaches, to be de-scribed later in this chapter, supplement your personal observations with the judgment of a professional and the results of psychological tests. Even the professional counselor, however, will force you to make most of the discoveries about yourself. Whether you rely upon your own resources or supplement them with professional help, you will have to confront yourself about yourself. Why women seek self-knowledge is cogently summarized in a brochure, "Stop the World I Want to Get On," distributed by the Continuum Center for Women.

> You could call it a "quest in search of self," I suppose. I am look-ing for something: a new dimension in living, maybe? Something that would seem terribly important to me—creative, challenging, meaningful—and helpful both to myself and others. Something I can

sink my teeth into, come to grips with, and lose myself in. Something that would be my task, suited to my capabilities, and fulfilling my needs for self-expression. Something that would open doors of the mind and excite the imagination, too. Some area in which I can both find myself and give of myself. Whether the area will be in work, in learning, or new hobbies, or exposure to enrichment programs, or whatever—I do not know. That's why I'm here.

The Self-Knowledge Questionnaire, presented next, provides a convenient starting point in the quest for more systematic knowledge about yourself. Some questions call for factual knowledge, others for attitudes and feelings. Questions in this latter category require more soul searching and pondering. Advice and suggestions from friends or husbands can be helpful in completing the Self-Knowledge Questionnaire. The sample form shown here has been completed by a thirty-year-old women. She later went on to reach some of the goals and plans she alludes to in her responses.

SELF-KNOWLEDGE QUESTIONNAIRE

Name: Doris Richards

Age: 30

I. Education

1. How far have I gone in school?
   College graduate, BA in history.
2. When did I last attend school?
   Graduated ten years ago.
3. Which were my best subjects?
   History, English, political science, archery.
4. Which were my poorest subjects?
   Chemistry, statistics, analytical geometry.
5. What night or adult education courses have I attended?
   Speed reading, history of the motion film.
6. What skills or abilities do I have now that could be applied to a job situation?
   I'm not sure. I read well and I can write OK. I'm good at listening to other people's problems.
7. What further educational plans do I have? Why?
   Maybe some courses in sociology, guidance, or psychology. Maybe I could qualify to be a caseworker or a social worker.

8. How much time would I have available for course work?
   One or two nights per week.
9. How would my husband and children feel about my attending school?
   My husband thinks it would be a good idea. Both my children would prefer to have me around all the time, but they can adjust.
10. Do I have the ability to take college courses?
    Absolutely. I had close to a B average in college. I got an A in the last course I took.

II. Work Experience
11. What jobs have I held since age sixteen?
    Two years selling Fanny Farmer candy during high school. Dining room hostess for three summers. While my husband was in the Army I wrote women's column for post newspaper.
12. What aspect of these jobs did I enjoy? Why?
    Seeing the women's column completed was a kick because I felt I really followed through on something. Interviewing people to get material for my column was very good. I don't like to use clichés, but "people are interesting."
13. What aspect of these jobs did I dislike? Why?
    Selling candy to old ladies. They treated me as if I were a slave or a child.
14. What kind of an employee was I?
    I was mediocre at selling candy. I thought I put together a first-rate newspaper column.
15. What compliments did I receive from bosses or co-workers?
    Hard worker, friendly.
16. What criticisms or suggestions did I receive?
    At the newspaper they said I was on the opinionated side.
17. What would be an ideal job for me?
    A high government official in the Department of Health Education and Welfare. I would be helping people but would also be in a glamorous, exciting position.

III. Attitudes Toward People
18. The kind of people I get along best with are:

Modern in their thinking. More liberal than conservative.
Not too pompous or stuffy. People who listen to
my opinions are the best!

19. The kind of people I clash with are:
People who try and put me down. Old-fashioned people
who say "a woman's place is in the home."

20. How many close friends do I have? What is it I like
about each one?
Three. Joanne and I are real close but we aren't too
dependent on each other. We don't "smother" each other.
Marge is the best listener I have ever known. Rhea's
sweet, nice, generous. She is just a real wonderful friend.

21. Would I prefer working mostly with men or women?
Men, as long as they treated me as an intellectual equal.

22. How much contact with other people do I need?
I need contact with adults everyday. I'm not the research
mole type.

23. My arguments with other people are mostly about:
Today's young people. I think they are real cool.
Some of my friends question their loyalty to our country.

IV. Attitudes Toward Myself

24. What are my strengths?
I'm smart. Attractive. I laugh a lot. I'm a good listener.
I'm well read. Honesty.

25. What are my weaknesses?
I'm sarcastic. I yell too much. I'm not the neatest
housekeeper. I'm not really very self-confident.

26. What do I worry about the most?
Whether or not I'm leading the best possible life for myself.

27. What is my biggest problem?
Finding myself in life.

28. What things in my life do I dislike?
Household chores. Having to argue with my children
about the same things all the time.

29. What have I accomplished in life so far?
I've raised two beautiful children. I've brought some
happiness to my parents and husband. I graduated
from college.

30. Has this been enough accomplishment?
    Definitely no!
31. What was the happiest period in my life? Why?
    The first two or three years of my marriage. I thought that this was the ideal way of life.
32. What gives me satisfaction in life?
    Some things about my husband and children and my friends. Money and possessions aren't as important.
33. In what ways do I punish myself?
    Sometimes I provoke an argument with my husband just before an important day like our anniversary. Then I'm miserable for most of that day.
34. What motivates me?
    The hope that I can become a bigger and better person.

V. How Others See Me
35. What is the best compliment my husband has paid me?
    He once said I was a person of depth.
36. In what ways would my husband like me to change?
    He thinks I shouldn't argue so much about topics unless I really know what I'm talking about.
37. What do other people like best about me?
    I listen to their problems without judging them.
38. What do other people dislike about me?
    Sometimes I'm too honest. If I don't agree with people, I tell them.

VI. Hobbies, Interests, Sports
39. What activities, hobbies, interests, sports, etc., do I actively participate in?
    Bridge, skiing, fiction and nonfiction reading, cub scout den mother, listen to music, follow movies.
40. Which ones of these do I really get excited about? Why?
    Skiing, it's really a wild feeling to make a run down a trail. It puts me close to nature. Bridge is also good for me. I play better than most of my friends, so I feel self-confident when I'm playing bridge.

VII. My Future
41. What goals or plans in life do I have?

a. Education and training.
I want to take a course of study that will qualify me to be a social worker.

b. Career and job.
Become a good social worker. Actually help lots and lots of people who need help.

3. Activities and interests.
I have enough of those. Maybe take up yoga seriously. I have heard that yoga can put your life on a whole new plane.

d. Plans and goals related to other people.
Maybe now is the time in life to find a way to improve communications between my husband and myself.
Provide for my children's education. Help them be happy.

Part VII of the Questionnaire focuses a woman's attention upon that part of her life wherein most of the opportunities for self-fulfillment lie—the future. Confident, positive, and interesting people orient a substantial proportion of their thinking toward the future. Insipid, vacuous, and uninspiring people focus most of their attention on the past. (Senility, of course, represents an exception. Reminiscing is an excusable preoccupation of the senile.) Present-oriented people lie somewhere in between these two extremes. Their thoughts are less than inspirational but they at least find some satisfaction in their private world as it exists today. Betty Friedan has illuminated the importance of goal setting in relation to personal growth: "A woman today who has no goal, no ambition patterning her days into the future, making her stretch and grow beyond that small score of years in which her body can fill its biological function, is committing a kind of suicide."[3]

Establishing goals contributes to an enlarged or strengthened self-image in one other vital way, as inferred by Charles A. Reich in *The Greening of America.* Changing goals, according to his analysis, is equivalent to having a new concept of oneself.[4] One woman in her early forties established a personal goal of educational enrichment. She enrolled in college and became a classmate of many persons equivalent in age to her oldest son. Her self-image shifted toward that of a more modern, psychologically younger person. Toward this end she lost weight and dressed in a fashion more appropriate to the times and her new environment. Positive changes took place within this woman stemming from the new goals she had established for herself.

Goal setting should precede actual implementation of approaches to self-improvement. The paths to self-fulfillment come into clearer focus when they are seen through the lens of carefully articulated goals and ambitions. Earl Nightingale, in one of his radio broadcasts, made the following prophetic statement. "Tell me what it is that you want, and I'll show you how to get it." Professional counselors are often best equipped to help you define "what it is that you want" and equally important, help you acquire some knowledge about the options available to you.

Counseling Helps Life Planning

Professional counseling carries several steps further the self-discovery process described so far. Life planning is strengthened by basing decisions about your future on as much information as possible. Counseling approaches to life planning, in general, rely on at least three sources of information: your evaluation and opinions about yourself, psychological test information, and judgments by the psychologist-counselor. Many women, away from a school or job environment for a number of years, develop almost phobic reactions to the prospects of taking psychological tests. They fear the embarrassment of "failing" an aptitude test. In reality, aptitude test results are used merely to help understand a person's strengths and weaknesses. Information obtained by the counselor is held in strict confidence and revealed only to the person being counseled and perhaps other professional personnel on the staff.

"Investigation Into Identity," a program by the Continuum Center for Women at Oakland University, represents a comprehensive and carefully developed approach to life planning geared specifically for women seeking a transition toward a more meaningful life. The housewife syndrome is the force motivating many women to enter this program. Divorcees and widows forced by circumstances to reorient their life style are also well represented among its clientele. Fees for the program are modest because the Kellogg Foundation underwrites approximately two thirds of the total cost.

"Investigation Into Identity" is a ten-session program geared toward self-evaluation and life planning. Women are encouraged to gain as much information about themselves as possible. Some of this self-evaluation is similar in format to the Self-Knowledge Questionnaire described earlier. Ample opportunity is provided for women to exchange information and feelings in group discussion. For many it is a revelation that other women are grappling with the same types of problems. In the words of one housewife,

> The big thing for me, was the group—finding out that so many women felt just the way I did. They loved their husbands and children, but they needed more in life. And *they* were nice women, so maybe there wasn't anything wrong with me. I could be a good wife and mother and still want something besides putting up peaches and going to the PTA. I started feeling better right then. And when my tests showed that I had the ability to go back to college, I felt like my life was being given back to me . . .[5]

Psychological testing provides the basic framework underlying each woman's investigation into her identity. Testing provides information about academic abilities, educational and occupational interests, personal values and preferences, and insights about her personality traits and characteristics. Psychologists have primary responsibility for interpreting test results, but the data are also discussed in groups with other women in the program. Sylvia Nelson, a forty-three-year-old college graduate with one teen-age child, exemplifies a person who finds the testing phase of the program particularly helpful:

> I had no confidence that I could do anything . . . I said I'd help with the Torch Drive, and then I chickened out. I didn't want to stand up in front of a group and speak . . .
> I was scared when I took the tests . . . and the day I had my date with the psychologist who evaluated them for me I actually shook. And what he told me! I'd always thought I was a loner, that I didn't like people, didn't relate. But he said that I had good social skills. Well, since then I've changed entirely. Maybe it was just being told I had some social skills, that I *did* get along with people. I found myself liking women for the first time. And my husband says he likes me better too. I'm still afraid to get up in front of a group of people and talk—but I do it. I made a promise to myself to do everything I'm afraid of . . . You have to risk to live.[6]

Psychologists have primary responsibility for the direction of each woman's program but assistance is also provided by specialists in the field of education, volunteer service, and employment. Interaction with the psychologist or any other of these specialists might be described as counseling in its broadest definition. Individual counseling is the most helpful phase of the program to some women. Barbara Hoffman, a forty-three-year-old woman whose family life suffered because she attempted to run a full-time lamp-making business and manage a home, recounts the following experience:

> I resisted enrolling at first . . . I thought that as a grown-up mature woman I should be able to figure out for myself what to do. I knew I had some talents and I didn't think it should be too difficult to decide what to do with them. So I sloshed around making myself more miserable until I finally joined the program. It changed my whole life. . . . She (the employment counselor) explained that other women are in the same boat. She even got five of us at the center together, and we formed a group to display our things . . . It's very important for a woman to know what to do with her skills. Otherwise, even though she knows she has some wisdom, some ability, it's like being all dressed up with no place to go.[7]

What kind of report might a psychologist prepare about a woman to assist her in life planning? Several different formats exist; the report style used in the "Investigation Into Identity" program is informal in tone and expressed in terms meaningful to the client. An important distinction must be drawn between a psychodiagnostic report written about a mentally ill woman and a counseling report. Counseling reports, in general, focus more upon behavior and skills than upon underlying personality traits or unconscious motivations. Women with serious emotional problems usually have to work through these first before life planning can achieve effective results. When it appears obvious to the counseling psychologist that a woman is emotionally ill, she is usually referred to a mental health facility (e.g. an appointment with a private psychiatrist). Again, the variety of counseling we refer to in this chapter is geared toward normal women seeking psychological growth. Chapter 9, "Discontent or Disturbed?" will explore further the difference between mental illness and the problems of normal women. The following report has been written about a woman who sought assistance in her life planning.

PSYCHOLOGICAL REPORT

Name: Maxine L. Gordon   Age: 36
Date: February 23, 1971
Psychologist: Robert J. Osburne

Interview Impressions

Mrs. Gordon is an attractive, soft-spoken woman in her middle thirties. She appears to be an individual who has had a great need to be honest in her interpersonal relationships and, additionally, impressed me as a humble and genuine person.

All three of her children are enrolled in school. This is the first time in many years that Mrs. Gordon has been able to "see daylight." Previous constraints consisted of her husband's seemingly jealous attitude and her consequent inability to engage in a variety of activities outside of the home. Secondly, she has been responsible for the care of an aging parent. These pressures combined with the usual demands of child rearing and homemaking have limited the amount of time she has been able to devote to her personal developemnt.

At this point, Mrs. Gordon seems quite excited about this newfound "daylight" and is interested in fully exploring the opportunities available to her—especially employment. She has engaged in a wide variety of activities outside the home despite these constraints on her time. Her activities have included serving as a volunteer authenticator of antiques for a local museum. The possibility of employment in the artistic area is very exciting to her and she hopes to fully explore this with the Education Advisor.

Mrs. Gordon's schedule will be quite busy until this summer. In the interim she is taking one course at a community college, and will also participate in several conferences with the Employment Advisor. Overall, Maxine Gordon impresses me as a bright woman who will be capable of a wide variety of educational or employment situations and who seemingly has strong needs to participate in something meaningful at this point. Her plan seems quite thorough and cautious and she will probably need a gentle nudge to activate herself in any activity. Her interpersonal skills will be a major plus in an employment situation. Perhaps we could also use this woman's talents as a discussion leader in our center.

Summary of Test Results

Her general level of mental ability is above average in comparison to college students. She has particularly well developed verbal skills. Her more strongly developed personality traits are imagination, self-sufficiency, and tender-mindedness. She has strong desires for working with ideas and directing other people. Her interest in literary or artistic occupational pursuits is pronounced and she has negative interests in clerical work.

Women who do not have access to the "Investigation Into Identity" program can find counseling assistance elsewhere. One example is the Career Guidance Seminar of Rochester Institute of Technology offered through the Office of Continuing Studies for Women at that school. Counseling centers of most universities offer some career guidance service to the public. Organizations such as the Personnel Psychology Center in New York City can be helpful. Some psychologists in private practice provide help in career planning as well as personal counseling and psychotherapy. Accredited psychologists are all members of the American Psychological Association and most states and provinces have certification or licensing laws governing the practice of psychology. Your state psychological association is a convenient source of information about the availability of testing services.

Psychological counseling and testing helps most, but not all, women in formulating plans for a higher level of self-fulfillment. Help is never guaranteed and most of the burden falls upon the woman for making psychological assistance a meaningful life experience. My observation is that approximately 70 to 80 percent of people who enter a counseling and testing program with a positive attitude derive some benefit from the experience. Harm from such a venture into self-knowledge occurs in miniscule proportion. Deleterious consequences to the woman from counseling would require a singularly ineffective counselor.

Your Commitment Must Be Serious

Women attempting to make the transition from apathy and indifference toward life to excitement and enthusiasm must do more than dabble at some activity they decide to undertake. Serious commitment is necessary. Taking a course in western civilization as a cure for the housewife syndrome for example, only aggravates the problem if you merely go through the motions of taking the course. Until an educational curriculum comes to mean more to you than a pleasant pastime, self-fulfillment will not be forthcoming. Similarly the woman who decides that acquiring competence in tennis will help strengthen her self-image will only weaken her self-image if she dabbles at the activity. Competence in tennis, similar to competence in any complex skill, requires diligence and application. Learning to play tennis well involves considerable frustration and hard work. Strengthened self-images arise from the learning of difficult tasks and the overcoming of obstacles. Activities of broader social significance than sports also have to be pursued with commitment and involvement in order to enhance your self-image. Dilettantes run the risk of frustration and perpetual boredom.

Betty Friedan highlights the importance of serious commitment in her plea for a new life plan for women:

> One woman I interviewed had involved herself in an endless whirl of worthwhile community activities. But they led in no direction to her own future, nor did they truly utilize her exceptional intelligence. Indeed, her intelligence seemed to deteriorate; she suffered the problem that has no name with increasing severity until she took the first step toward a serious commitment. Today she is a master teacher, a serene wife and mother.[8]

Commitment does not develop automatically, nor can it be achieved by simple desire. Some amount of trial and error and experimentation will be necessary before you discover activities to which you can commit yourself. It is important to stay with a given activity or experience long enough to adequately determine if commitment is possible. Becoming a market research interviewer on a part-time basis might represent the kind of experience you need to strengthen your self-image and raise your level of life satisfaction. Rejecting market research as an avenue of self-fulfillment because of the first unsuccessful interview would be unfair to yourself. Effort must be applied and hurdles must be overcome before commitment can be developed. Many women emotionally commit themselves to skiing (to use a hobby analogy) even though their first attempts at skiing were psychologically and physically painful. Learning to ski involves a continuous sequence of overcoming small hurdles and learning new skills.

Selecting a course of action of appropriate difficulty level is a key factor in developing commitment. The housewife who decides that her path to self-fulfillment requires the writing of a best-selling novel is inviting frustration, disappointment, and lack of commitment, unless she is a person of rare and exceptional talent. Attempting to develop commitment to raising goldfish, on the other hand, may also lead to despair and lack of commitment, but for different reasons. Tasks that are too easy and not psychologically meaningful to an individual will also fail to provide a vehicle for strengthening the self-image.

Practice Good Mental Health

People with good psychological adjustment—those who might be described as "emotionally healthy"—have strong self-images. The opposite is also true; people with strong self-images have good psychological adjustment. Whether a strong self-image emerges because you practice good mental health, or good mental health occurs because you have a strong self-image is mostly of academic interest. Either way, the woman attempting to make the transition toward self-fulfillment must practice good mental health. Laurance F. Shaffer and Edward J. Shoben, Jr., two psychologists at Columbia University, formulated a list of conditions for mental health that have withstood the test of time.[9] Many of these principles or suggestions reinforce what has already been mentioned in the context of improved life planning. These principles do not invariably bring improved mental health to their adherents, nor are they easy to follow. The psychology of adjustment cannot offer exact prescriptions for mental health, nor are people always in a position to control their own behavior or modify their environment. However, to the extent that a woman adheres to the following principles, there is a high probability that her self-image will be strengthened and her *transition* facilitated.

Good Physical Health. Physical condition has an obvious effect upon mental and emotional health. People preoccupied with concerns about their physical condition cannot focus their attention upon the gratification of higher-level psychological needs. Women embarking upon a campaign of self-improvement should begin with a thorough physical examination for important but subtle reasons. Physical ailments, fatigue, headaches, overweight, underweight, and tender gastrointestinal systems are frequetnly proffered as defenses against pursuing a program of self-development. "How can I figure out what to do with my spare time until I cure my physical problems?" is not an atypical defense against the efforts required in self-development. One vital contribution a physician can make to a woman's development is to convince her that her problems are *not physical in origin.* Physical culturalists, sports enthusiasts, and other outdoor types attest to the value of regular exercise for improving mental health. Informal observation suggests they are correct. Women in good physical condition look better to others and feel better to themselves. Those in poor physical condition frequently worry about their physical distress, thus impairing rather than enhancing mental health.

Accepting Yourself. Well-adjusted people live comfortably with themselves. This does not infer a smug complacency (which blocks personal growth) but a realistic acceptance of one's own strengths and limitations. The self-accepting woman is not shocked to find that she has personal limitations but accepts these and uses them as guideposts to personal development. Self-acceptance is not an easy attitude to develop if one has been practicing self-rejection since childhood. Steps can be taken to increase your level of self-acceptance. The major task in acquiring self-acceptance is understanding yourself. Although we have previously commented upon this notion, it bears repeating. First, you need to know how you operate, what your major desires are, and how you go about satisfying them. Second, you have to recognize your strengths and successes without belittling yourself if they are in short supply. Third, you must face your limitations, failures, and mistakes without too much need for self-deceit and rationalization. Learning to step back and poke fun at your mistakes and hang-ups is a useful tool for achieving self-acceptance.

Accepting Other People. Understanding of other people, according to Shaffer and Shoben, has an importance for mental health second only to understanding yourself.[10] Acceptance of others implies that you both understand them and tolerate their attitudes and views. More, total acceptance of others also implies a warm liking for them. To achieve acceptance of others you must first take an objective (nonsubjective or unbiased) look at their strengths, limitations, and points of view. Liberals, for example, are not necessarily any more accepting of others than are conservatives. Acceptance of others implies a willingness to at least listen to a point of view that differs from your own perception of the world. Acceptance of others is blocked more frequently by a real or implied threat from others than by any other single factor. Women most intolerant toward lesbians, following this logic, usually have some inner fears that they would enjoy succumbing to their own lesbian desires. Similarly, the people most vehemently opposed to blacks being granted special privileges are white semiskilled workers—precisely that group most likely to be displaced by black entrants into nonmenial jobs.

Maintain a Confidential Relationship. Many people welcome long-term psychotherapy simply out of emotional loneliness. This is not to discredit this function of the therapist. Confidants, whether they take the form of spouse, lover, lawyer, physician, bartender, psychotherapist, or friend, are important for the maintenance of good mental health. The value of a confidant usually stems not from the advice they give, but their ability to allow you to express feeling without their passing judgment.

This is the era of confrontation and openness. Less time is therefore required than in times past to form confidential relationships with people. Adaptation to transient communities has required that people form close relationships in a short period of time in order to preserve mental health. Despite this trend toward openness, there is a danger in sharing intimacies with others before they understand you well enough to enter into a confidential relationship with you. Women in search of an intimate friend often try too hard and move too quickly. Second meetings with another person, as one case in point, are rarely the time to divulge financial or marital problems. Sensitivity to the readiness of other people to serve as your confidant is also an important characteristic for forming satisfying, confidential relationships with people.

Action Must Be Taken. Maintenance of good mental health requires more than talking about problems. Admittedly there is *some* benefit in merely discussing feelings, attitudes, and apprehensions with a confidant, but equally important, something constructive must be done about the problem. Even when an attempt at problem resolution does not succeed entirely some anxiety is reduced by the active effort alone. Overweight individuals, it has been observed, feel less anxious and uncomfortable about their physical problem merely by enrolling in an organization devoted to weight reducing. The problem of obesity has not yet been overcome, but one important psychological step in the right direction has been taken. In short, you have to do something constructive about your problems, not just ruminate and introspect.

Interaction with People. Interacting with other people is more conducive to good mental health than engaging in solitary activities. The aphorism offered to the lonely, "Get out and meet people," contains a modicum of truth. Placed in a group setting, people tend to be less preoccupied with their personal concerns. Attending to the words of other people focuses your attention on something other than your own reveries. Additionally, social interaction provides you the opportunity to practice other requirements for good mental health such as acceptance of others and taking action about your problems. Women, perhaps even more so than males, enjoy small group activities. Interacting with people, thus, is a relatively natural form of good mental health practice for the majority of women.

Meaningful Work. Considerable experimental evidence and opinion exists attesting to the importance of meaningful work to good mental health. Many of the problems of housewives alluded to in Chapter 1 stem from the fact that homemaking has relatively low social status. What constitutes meaningful work to one woman might be considerably less meaningful to another. Practical nursing, to cite one occupation, might represent satisfaction and self-fulfillment to a forty-five-year-old woman with strong needs to help people and low interest in working with theoretical ideas. People with at least average intelligence and education usually consider work meaningful that provides recognition, a sense of accomplishment, and opportunities for advancement. Women reorienting themselves to the world of work will need careful planning to find such work. Chapter 6, "Venture into the World Outside," will explore this matter in more depth.

Creative Experience. Deep satisfactions are forthcoming to the woman who can look upon any aspect of her life as a *creative experience.* Feelings such as these contribute directly to positive mental health. Individuals arrive at their personal definition of what constitutes creativity. However, one important component of a creative experience is the opportunity to choose your task and set your goals. The standard of excellence can be defined by you. Opportunities for creative experience do not abound within the basic housewife role, although they exist for some women. Interior decorating and clothes designing are two examples. Despite such exceptions, women usually have to look beyond the confines of their homes to find such creative outlets. Successful life planning takes this factor into account.

Use the Scientific Method. Perhaps the most general principle of good mental health practice is to use the scientific method to solve personal problems. The same approach that scientists use to arrive at solutions to complex problems can be successfully applied to your personal situation. Susan Whipple, to cite one situation, decides she is basically unhappy with her role in life. As a first step she gathers data to carefully define the problem. She asks the opinions of her husband and children about whether or not she appears unhappy. She also asks if there are ways in which she is letting down or disappointing them. Secondly, Sue formulates the tentative hypothesis that although she is performing adequately as a wife and mother, she is a victim of the *housewife syndrome*. Thirdly, she examines various approaches to overcoming this condition. After careful life planning she selects one goal—to become a mutual fund sales representative—and pursues this goal with diligence and vigor. If this plan fails, rather than surrender she takes a new approach. In the words of Shaffer and Shoben, "When you can secure a balanced satisfaction of your motives by planned courses of action, you will have achieved integrated adjustment and satisfying living, which is good mental health."[11]

Good mental health is difficult to achieve or maintain without proper support from other people. Husbands can contribute to both strengthening the self-image of their wives and creating an environment conducive to good mental health.

Husbands Must Cooperate

Whatever new life plans you develop or whatever new measures you take to practice better mental health, your plans will proceed more smoothly if your husband offers his cooperation and support. Healthy, well-integrated, nonthreatened males welcome spouses with strengthened self-images. Less healthy, less integrated, and more insecure males consciously and unconsciously place roadblocks in the paths of their wives' self-development. Cooperation by the husband occurs at two levels: the physical or financial, and the emotional or psychological.

Physical and financial cooperation by the husband includes his willingness to allocate family funds to matters such as school tuition, increased baby-sitting costs, and the purchase of items related to new interests. Women whose self-development requires time away from home may want a husband to devote more time than usual to child rearing and basic household tasks.

Emotional and psychological support is possibly more important than physical and financial support. Self-development can be sabotaged by a husband who resents his wife's strengthening her self-image. Husbands exist who protect their own ego by deliberately squashing that of their wife. "Don't be surprised if the other students in the class call you Mom," said one husband with antagonistic attitudes toward his wife's returning to college. This kind of reaction to a woman's pursuit of development, if it occurs frequently, forces her to choose between loyalty to herself and loyalty to her husband. Psychological support for a woman's endeavors in self-improvement manifests itself in positive and enthusiastic responses to her activities. Simple declarative statements such as "Sheila, you must feel good about receiving two job offers" communicates in a meaningful way that the husband stands behind his wife's development.

"Marital teams" is the name for the new life style that enables women to participate as fully as men in society. Under this arrangement husbands and wives jointly share work and family responsibilities. Many marital teams originated with couples who met at a university, typically when both were graduate students. In this unique situation husbands and wives are forced by necessity to share equally in earning a living and tending to the mechanics of running a household. One husband-wife graduate student team arranged their class schedule in different shifts in order to cope with child rearing. When the woman attended class or did her research at the library, the husband tended their infant child. Roles were reversed when the husband had to attend class or work in the library. This kind of team arrangement has enough appeal to some couples to be extended beyond the graduate student phase of their life. Husbands participating in marital team arrangements provide both physical and psychological support to a woman's quest for self-fulfillment and an identity of her own.

Male proponents of the women's liberation movement have demonstrated total support for their wives' pursuit of self-development and self-fulfillment. Eugene Heidi, whose wife is active in the National Organization of Women, is one such male. He reports, "We relate to each other as individual human beings, each person strong in his own identity . . . I have experienced role reversal many times when I've stayed home and done the housework while Wilma worked. This bothers a lot of men, but it's never been an ego problem for me."[12]

Husbands, in addition to providing assistance to wives in their pursuit of self-development, can also play a key role in enabling a woman to practice good mental health. Self-images, as discussed earlier, tend to be strengthened under the conditions of authentic and open interpersonal relationships. Spouses, if for no other reason than their physical proximity, represent a logical partner with whom to participate in such relationships.

Assume that a woman has successfully carved out a new life plan designed to strengthen her self-image, and has involved her husband in this plan. Still another important task remains to facilitate putting this plan into action—improving the basic homemaking task.

NOTES

1. Mary McSherry, "Help for 'just-a-housewife' Blues," *Woman's Day*, June 1970, p. 108.
2. Nanette E. Scofield and Betty Klarman, *So You Want to Go Back to Work*, New York, Random House, 1968, pp. 19-20.
3. Betty Friedan, *The Feminine Mystique*, New York, Dell, 1970.
4. Charles A. Reich, *The Greening of America: How the Youth Revolution Is Trying to Make America Livable*, New York, Random House, 1971.
5. Mary McSherry, *op. cit.*, p. 106.
6. *Ibid.*, p. 107.
7. *Ibid.*, p. 107.
8. Betty Friedan, *op. cit.*, p. 333.
9. Laurance F. Shaffer and Edward J. Shoben, Jr., *The Psychology of Adjustment*, Boston, Houghton Mifflin, 1956.
10. *Ibid.*, p. 587.
11. *Ibid.*, p. 590.
12. Jurate Kazickas, "Lib Husbands Living with the Movement," *Democrat & Chronicle*, Rochester, New York, Jan. 24, 1971, p. 5E.

Chapter 5

IMPROVING THE HOMEMAKING TASK

Some respite to husbands
the weather may send,
But housewives' affairs
have never an end.

Preface to
Book of Housewifery

How Do Homemakers Spend Their Time?

Women in pursuit of self-development and self-fulfillment are rarely in a position to entirely eliminate homemaking tasks from their daily repertoire of activities. Even women of substantial financial resources have to devote some time to household chores. Married, divorced, separated, widowed, and single women all spend some time at the mechanics of daily living. Homemakers are not alone in this regard. Every occupation has its routine, straightforward, nonglamorous components. Company presidents have to devote time to committee meetings that are often uninspiring, petty, and mentally fatiguing. College professors, as further illustration, spend some time in routine matters such as grading examinations and haggling with students about grades. Any plans you develop for increasing your life satisfaction or strengthening your self-image will proceed more swiftly once you find more efficient methods of dispensing with the routine, uninspiring aspects of your role.

Improving any task begins with an analysis of the components of that task. Several attempts have been made to analyze the amount and distribution of time devoted to homemaking responsibilities. Every woman conducts her activities with individual variation and few women feel they should be characterized as "average." Statistical studies, however, have some merit as starting points for dis-

TABLE I

HOURS PER WEEK DEVOTED TO HOUSEHOLD TASKS

Household Task	1920	1952	1968	1970
Meal preparation and dishwashing	13.3	17.5	18.5	20.0
Clothing care (washing, ironing, sewing)	8.6	10.5	7.3	8.3
House care	7.3	9.8	10.8	12.0
Family care	9.5	5.6	6.4	8.8
Management and shopping	5.5	4.2	4.1	4.4
Yard work	—	—	.6	.7
Chauffeuring	—	—	1.4	1.6
Miscellaneous	4.6	—	.4	.5
Total hours per week	48.8	47.6	49.5	56.3

cussion. Two home economists prepared a comparison of the time spent on household tasks at different time points in recent history.[1] Several conclusions are apparent from this analysis presented in Table I. First, modern conveniences and appliances have had a negligible effect upon the amount of time women devote to household tasks. Electric ranges, as one example, may enable homemakers to cook with more precision but the amount of time devoted to meal preparation has actually increased over the years. Second, with the assistance of more effective methods of cleaning house, women have raised their standards of cleanliness in lieu of decreasing the amount of time devoted to housecleaning. Automatic car washes provide an analogous situation. More time is probably devoted to car washing now than in the past, simply because better methods of car washing (automatic car washes) are now available. Third, homemakers spend about as much time at household tasks as professional and managerial people do at their respective occupational roles.

Estimates such as these about the long hours of homemaking have not gone unchallenged. Betty Friedan writes passionately that "housewivery expands to fill the time available."[2] Women who have commitments in life beyond homemaking require less time to accomplish the same amount of work. Simply stated, if housework is not your main job, you tend to get it accomplished more quickly. Women who study the problems of other women have told me that four hours per day represents a true estimate of the amount of time required to perform household tasks. This figure assumes a "normal" family situation with two children beyond the infant stage and a moderate-sized house.

One professional man took over household responsibilities during a two-week period in which his wife was hospitalized. He commented, "Now I understand why Linda is so uptight. If I had a job that took only three hours a day to do efficiently, I'd wonder what to do with my time also."

Lillian Baxter works as the personal secretary to the dean of her college and also supervises the work of three other secretaries. She, by informal title, is both a supervisor and administrative assistant. Lillian accomplishes most of her job responsibilities during the normal work week but uses an occasional Saturday or Sunday to stay on top of peak-load situations. Running her home constitutes a sideline for Lillian. A home economics professor inquired about how she manages this dual role as career woman and homemaker. She replied:

> Simple; here's how it works. Before I leave in the morning at eight, I get some of the minor things done. Each night I get home at about five. My husband comes home around six thirty. This gives me an hour and one half to clean house, fix dinner and prepare cocktails. Then I have the whole night free after eight thirty to do what I please. As for your question about having a cleaning lady to help me, I would regard that as an insult. I should be able to manage my own home.

Few women have the personal organization, energy, or commitment of a Lillian Baxter, but an important principle of work psychology is suggested here. Women who are enthusiastic about something—be it some aspects of their housework, their careers, or their hobbies—will find ways to efficiently handle basic household tasks. Once these more mundane tasks are taken care of time is available for more meaningful life experiences. Effective people in any occupational role find efficient ways to conquer the more trivial requirements of their work. How to make the transition from preoccupation with trivia to concentration on the more meaningful parts of the homemaker's role constitutes the key subject matter of this chapter.

The Candy House Orgasm

Some activities related to the homemaking function provide more opportunities for creative outlet than do others. The following anecdote about three suburban housewives illustrates the intellectual and artistic excitement that can occur within the context of a homemaker's role.

> Each Christmas, for three consecutive years, two women collaborated in the making of Christmas candy houses. Building the candy house required one full evening's activity. The "house" in reality was a winter scene with small plastic animals, green gumdrops for hedges, chocolate bars for doors, and pocket mirrors for ponds. Children marveled at the completed project; and the two collaborators on the project derived considerable gratification of their creative urges through its construction. The charm of the candy house became well known within the neighborhood.
>
> For the fourth year, a close friend of the originators of the candy house was brought in as a third member of the project. Paula, the new member, became enthralled with the beauty and artistic merit of her finished project. Feeling less and less inhibited as the evening of drinking and creativity progressed, she became more and more vocal in her statements of the merit of her candy house. Her breathing suddenly began to quicken. "Oh oh," said one of the other two women, "I think Paula is going to have an orgasm over her candy house."

Few homemaking tasks have such potency, but there is evidence that some homemaking tasks are considered more favorably than others by most women. Each woman may have her particular list of what constitutes a more desirable (or perhaps less undesirable) homemaking activity, but one general principle seems to underlie these preferences. To the extent that a woman perceives a particular task as providing some outlet for her inherent creativity, that task is viewed favorably. What constitutes a suitable outlet for creativity or self-expression is not the same for all women. Many women consider gardening as creative, relaxing, and even therapeutic. Gardening to others is an uncomfortable, even burdensome activity. The following classification of household tasks according to their desirability is based upon research conducted with upstate New York housewives.[3]

The list of desirable and undesirable household tasks contained in Table II reflects simply how women feel about these activities. Your particular preferences may differ. Generalizing broadly, it can be said that few women will find much opportunity for creative expression in the "Mostly Undesirable" list, while many women

TABLE II

DESIRABLE AND UNDESIRABLE HOMEMAKING TASKS

Mostly Desirable	*Mostly Undesirable*
Hostessing parties	Cleaning bathroom
Interior decorating	Washing floors
Activities with children	Cleaning kitchen
Preparing holiday meals	Disciplining children
Bed making	Ironing clothes
Gardening	Home bookkeeping
Grocery shopping	Cleaning woodwork

find satisfaction in those activities classified as "Mostly Desirable." For you to substantially improve the homemaking task, you must eliminate, delegate, or deemphasize those items in your personal "Mostly Undesirable" list.

Entire elimination of a given homemaking chore is admittedly difficult; exceptions are few but important. Reducing or eliminating ironing by proper utilization of permanent-press clothing is the most frequently cited labor-saving measure. Washing floors is an activity that cannot be eliminated but that can readily be deemphasized or reduced by maneuvers such as using floor covering that does not readily show dirt. Specific labor- or time-saving hints for a given household task are a product of common sense. Daily newspapers forever have columns giving advice on such matters. Home economics, surprisingly, is a scant source of information on methods of more efficient homemaking. Courses in homemaking are oriented more toward occupations such as dietetics and food management than toward the concerns of individual homemakers. Hints on how to more efficiently accomplish a given household task, however, make only a moderate-sized contribution to improving the homemaking function. Reliance on this approach requires that you commit dozens of small hints to memory for occasional use. What is more important is the development of attitudes that compel you to question both *how* and *why* you are performing a particular activity.

Improving the homemaking task thus requires that the homemaker learn to challenge basic assumptions. Systems analysts (modern-day counterparts of efficiency experts) in organizational life owe much of their success to challenging assumptions that have previously gone unchallenged. Denise Falls is a homemaker with three children; her situation illustrates the concept of *challenging basic assumptions* in regard to homemaking.

> Denise embarked upon a campaign of improving homemaking in order to increase her enjoyment of day-by-day living. Her list of undesirable homemaking tasks centered around spending large amounts of time in the kitchen, particularly when she might better devote the time to playing golf or joining in activities with her children. Denise's problem is familiar to many busy people. Where do you cut? What activity can you eliminate? Carefully reviewing her weekly schedule, Denise noticed that much of her weekend time was consumed by activities related to meal preparation. Following the *challenge basic assumptions approach,* Denise asked herself and her husband, "Why do we have Sunday dinners? Why not a light, informal supper that requires little preparation?"
>
> Several responses to this question were "Sunday is the day of the week when families gather together . . . Our family has always had big dinners on Sunday . . . It's the proper thing to do on Sunday . . . We have Sunday dinner because that's what families do on Sunday afternoon together . . . It must have something to do with religious observance."
>
> Denise then realized none of these reasons implied that large Sunday meals were a *necessity*. Perhaps family life would not be adversely affected, and might even improve, if the Sunday dinner tradition were replaced by a light informal supper that simultaneously provided Denise more time for golf and less time in the kitchen. Denise's husband was particularly enthusiastic. He responded, "That's a good idea, I never really liked being confined to the house on Sunday afternoon. I'm sure the children would rather spend time with their friends than with us on Sunday afternoon."

This anecdote illustrates the challenging of an obvious assumption. With some mental effort you can find less obvious assumptions to challenge. Most homemakers I have observed, for example, assume that all children require two sheets on their bed. Children grow equally well, physically and psychologically, if they use one sheet or sleeping-bag-like arrangements. The amount of time saved from not arranging, folding, washing, and ironing sheets can be substantial. Again, it is more important to develop the mental habit of learning to challenge basic assumptions than to learn "one thousand labor-saving tips for the homemaker." Generalizing further, the central, underlying ingredient of improving the homemaking task is for the homemaker to become a more effective manager.

Every Homemaker a Manager

Women who, by natural inclination or concentrated effort, apply principles of management to their homemaking responsibilities can at least reduce some of the frustrations in their role. By practicing these principles you may not receive the same degree of job satisfaction as a vice president in a large organization, but at least some of the burdensome elements associated with the homemaking can be reduced. Writers about management topics and managers themselves differ on what constitute the "principles of management." There are many different ways to define the managerial function and many of these differences appear to be problems of semantics. Managers, according to a convenient and widely used formulation plan, organize, control, lead, and innovate. These managerial functions can be explained in terms of their relevance to improving the homemaking task.

Planning refers to preparing for what is anticipated in the future; either single events or complex series of events such as living patterns may be planned. Vacation planning, to cite a familiar situation, involves such preparations as making hotel and airline reservations months in advance, setting aside funds to pay for the vacation, and arranging for pet and or child care for those who stay behind. Common symptoms of poor planning, or no planning at all, are waiting until light bulbs burn out to purchase new ones, having an empty whiskey cabinet on a Sunday, using your husband's last razor blade, and selling jewelry to pay for school tuition. Careful planning, in contrast, is illustrated by the woman who anticipates what household items she needs in advance and invests the time she saves by not running unnecessary errands into activities she enjoys.

Careful planning benefits the homemaker in another important way besides saving time, money, and energy. Planning, for many people, is an intrinsically enjoyable activity. For many managers, planning is the *fun* part of their job. In order to plan effectively, you have to devote effort to *thinking* rather than *doing*. Considerable self-discipline and determination is required to allot time for planning. According to one insightful principle of organizational theory, "Daily routine tends to drive out planning." In practice this means that you will allow minor tasks and interruptions to interfere with your making plans to deal more effectively with events that are to happen in the future. Any plan must allow room for unanticipated events (what do you do when a friend drops in unexpectedly and wants to chat with you about her marital problems for two hours?). Fifteen minutes per day should suffice for effective planning of homemaker responsibilities for most women.

What does planning involve in terms of its actual details? Generally it involves simply making lists of tasks that have to be performed, errands that have to be run, or steps that have to be taken to reach an end result. Many women experience a minor sense of accomplishment when they have completed the items on their plan for a particular day or week. Letty Cottin Pogrebin, public relations executive, author, and mother of three children, describes her approach to planning, "I'm a compulsive list maker . . . I make up all the menus and grocery list for the week every Saturday and lists of activities and places to go for the children and lists of all sorts of things to do."[4]

Planning can only be effective if the list is read and if items appearing on the list are accomplished. Some people err on the side of including all their daily activities on the list. Planning then becomes diary keeping, and the positive value of the list is lost.

Organizing, in the context of managerial principles, means arranging and assigning work in order to reach certain goals or objectives. Families are essentially small organizations in which different people perform different roles in order to reach objectives. Homemaking can be a less arduous chore when work areas (e.g. kitchens) are carefully laid out and when tasks are assigned to the appropriate people. Many homemaking tasks can be delegated to children—more than is commonly done in middle class homes. Adolescent children are not domestic servants but they are a convenient source of assistance if properly motivated.

One frequent problem in both larger organizations and in family units is overlapping of responsibility among its members. Ideally, most tasks can be handled by one family member. Bed making might be the responsibility of a fourteen-year-old boy or girl. Managing family finances, except for questions about major expenditures on which joint agreement is important, should be the sole responsibility of either the husband or wife. Bookkeeping and bed making as they apply to a family are not big enough jobs to be handled by more than one person. Two people managing finances in a family leads to confusion, unpaid bills, overdrawn accounts, and petty bickering.

Carrying the principle of organizing to its counterpart in a larger organization, the homemaker might list each person in the family along with his or her assigned homemaking tasks. In more technical terms, a job description might be written for each family member. Job titles might also be assigned, but this can lead to conflict. One woman protested during an interview about her role as a homemaker, "You can't really say that I'm in charge of the family. My husband won't admit to this but he acts as if he were the president and the controller. He puts me in the job of a foreman. I should have more power in the family structure."

Controlling in a management context means taking measurements to find out what results are happening and judge if things are occurring according to plans. Another form of control is to take measures to prevent unwanted acts from happening. Imposing limits on expense account privileges is an example of this latter type of control. Homemakers may find controlling less comfortable psychologically than other managerial functions. Ideally family members should learn to control their own behavior and not require controls or measurements by other people. Mothers inspecting to determine if children have washed their hands is one elemental form of control. Asking your husband to review with you family income and expenses for the last two months is a more subtle form of control.

Women frequently need to establish time controls for others in the family in order to preserve time for themselves. Children might be given strict limits on how much of the mother's time they can occupy in the evening. Husbands too must be made aware of what time belongs exclusively to the wife. This time, because of its scarcity, must be wisely invested in self-development or out-of-the-ordinary activities. Controls are also necessary to determine if those family members given assignments have carried them out properly or even done them. Family members sometimes welcome measurement of their assigned tasks, particularly if this measurement involves praise. Statements such as "Hey, Jim, that fence you built for us is really nice" are potent motivators for a husband or child to tackle another assignment in the future.

Controls and measures in the home, as well as within larger organizations, may be resented if not exercised with sensitivity. Children, for example, might respond better to controls if they make the decision as to when you will inspect their completed household chores. Husbands show less resentment when they participate in developing the limits you might try to impose on their behavior. Asking a husband how much time he needs or would like to spend on fishing per month might result in less time devoted to that activity than if you took the more authoritarian approach, "Henry, according to my demands, you can only spend six hours per week and three whole days per season on fishing."

Leading is the process of influencing people to achieve certain objectives, either those you or they establish. A strong component of leadership ability is required to effectively manage a household. Similarly a manager cannot rely exclusively upon the formal authority given to him by the organization. He must have a degree of personal appeal and form constructive relationships with subordinates in order to achieve company objectives. Viewed more simply, leadership is the interpersonal or social aspect of a manager's job. Homemakers must help create a psychological climate that encourages husbands and children to want to participate in the conduct of homemaking tasks.

Possessing leadership characteristics—particularly those such as warmth, compassion, and understanding—exerts a positive motivational impact upon others in the family. Firmness and decisiveness are also important leadership qualities for getting things accomplished through others, but may be more applicable to community and business than family leadership situations.

Counseling and coaching is another important aspect of the *leading* portion of management, and has some relevance for improving the homemaking task. Children (and perhaps husbands) often resist cooperating with household tasks simply because they lack appropriate skills in these areas. Children coached about how to make beds and gently counseled about their mistakes will normally show a willingness to try again for satisfactory performance. In contrast, an authoritarian approach to criticizing the mistakes of husbands and children when they attempt to help you will usually backfire. People, if it is within their control, will attempt to avoid situations that lead to personal criticism.

Innovating is expected of an effective manager. Managers who do not provide new and useful ideas to the group run the risk of being perceived as sterile administrators. Women who innovate in the context of homemaking profit in two important ways. First, innovativeness (or at least high-level common sense) is required to circumvent some of the more tedious aspects of a homemaker's role. You have to be clever to conjure up methods of simplifying your daily routine. Second, innovativeness even in its most elemental form furnishes some outlet for self-expression and creativity. As discussed earlier, such outlets make a positive contribution to your mental health.

Opportunities for innovativeness do not abound within the context of homemaking, but with proper motivation several possibilities can be found. Thinking of novel vacations, finding vehicles for improving communications within the family, preparing gourmet foods, inventing children's games, and thinking up new approaches to keeping children occupied on rainy days represent some avenues for innovation. Another important point about innovative ability should be kept in clear focus. Not all women who come up with clever ideas are inherently innovative. Part of being innovative is knowing how to borrow ideas from others and where to look for these new ideas. Many creative people are simply good synthesizers of other people's novel ideas.

Enthusiasm Makes You Efficient

Two broad strategies exist for making people more efficient in their work: the engineering and the motivational. According to the engineering approach, the tasks should be designed in such a manner that there is a minimum of wasted effort and motion. This concept is less than a new one and has served as a foundation for industrial engineering. F. B. Gilbreth showed at the turn of the century that the work of the average bricklayer can be increased from 120 to 350 bricks per hour by following a more efficient pattern of movement.[5] Time and motion studies have also at various times been applied to homemaking tasks. Two researchers at the University of Vermont did a serious study of bed making. Results showed that women walked distances such as 262 or 188 feet in making a bed. By beginning at the head of the bed and working around, it was possible to reduce the total distance walked to 23 feet and one inch.[6] Despite the time and energy saved in this method, it has had a minimal impact upon bed-making behavior of women and the study is rarely quoted.

In short, the engineering approach to efficiency of task performance attempts to compensate for individual differences in ability and motivation. Any person of normal intelligence and normal physical stamina can follow these methods and simplify his or her work. The major drawback to these approaches with almost every group but production workers is that they are resisted. Few people really want to follow a rigidly prescribed work pattern despite the energy and time they might save.

The second broad strategy for increasing efficiency in the performance of tasks is to capitalize upon the motivation and enthusiasm of people. Women can clean an entire four-bedroom house in two hours given the external motivation of preparing the house for a welcome visitor. Men can dramatically reduce the time required to mow a lawn given the incentive of something exciting to do after having completed cutting the grass. Properly motivated, almost any woman of normal physical stamina can quickly dispense with the repetitive and routine requirements of the homemaker role. Enthusiastic and well-motivated women are not controlled by homemaking chores. In contrast, *they* control these chores.

Wherein lie the wellsprings of this motivation and enthusiasm to overcome the mundane requirements of the homemaker role? The least probable source of this motivation stems directly from the housekeeping tasks. Some women, however infrequent among middle class, well-educated women, actually enjoy the process of housekeeping. Housework is a reward, not a punishment in their life. An extreme situation is shown by one middle-aged suburban housewife who devoted most of her energy in life to meticulous concern for housekeeping detail. Housecleaning was more important to her psychologically than her relationships with her husband or children. During the banter of a cocktail party her husband lamented, "The reason my sex life is so bad is that my wife doesn't want the sheets mussed."

Earlier the differentiation was drawn between desirable and undesirable homemaking tasks. Many women, fortunately for children, derive considerable personal satisfaction from child rearing. They genuinely regard interacting with children as both a challenge and a rewarding experience. Women with these attitudes can become enthusiastic about household chores because once these chores are out of the way, time is available for relating to children. Similarly, many teachers who enjoy the process of teaching speed through the paper-work requirements of their job so they can get on with teaching. One can become enthusiastic about the less desirable aspects of the homemaker role if you recognize that once these are taken care of, time is available for more rewarding activities. Distasteful chores then become more enjoyable because they represent minor hurdles that, once overcome, provide time for activities that lead to personal satisfaction. Developing the insight that "once I knock these petty chores over, I can get on with preparing that Polynesian dinner" serves as a potent source of energy.

Perhaps the most important and enduring well-spring of enthusiasm and energy for dispensing with homemaking tasks in an efficient manner stems from a commitment to things outside of homemaking. Rare in frequency, but important in principle, is the example of the homemaker who is also a novelist. If she budgets herself eight hours per week to work on her novel, she will manage her homemaker responsibilities in such a manner as to find those eight hours for her writing.

Women committed to things outside the home do not inevitably neglect homemaking chores. (Some women neglect housekeeping chores once they find something more interesting to occupy their time. This chapter, however, is written for women who *want* to improve the homemaking task.) They simply have enough enthusiasm and purpose in life to quickly overcome the hurdles to life satisfaction imposed by the mundane aspects of their roles. Women who make a commitment to a career, serious hobby, or education frequently become more efficient homemakers. In the process of commitment they have found a new source of energy and innovativeness to overcome the mechanics of daily living.

Clear distinction must be drawn between the genuine enthusiasm and motivation we have described and the delusional approach that is occasionally proffered as a solution to the housewife syndrome. This approach dictates that the homemaker delude herself into finding reward in every aspect of housekeeping. "How can I be unhappy when I see rainbows in every dishwater bubble?" exclaims the deluded homemaker. She, in the final analysis, is a candidate for both the housewife syndrome and perhaps psychosomatic symptoms. Thinly veiled delusions of this type cannot permanently protect a woman from her true feelings. According to the motivational approach recommended for women in transition, dishwashing should be regarded as one more picayune chore to be dispensed with efficiently in order to get on with the process of living.

NOTES

1. Florence T. Hall and Marguerite P. Schroeder, "Effect of Family and Housing Characteristics on Time Spent on Household Tasks," *Journal of Home Economics*, 62:23-29, Jan. 1970.
2. Betty Friedan, *The Feminine Mystique*, New York, Dell, 1970.
3. Gerald R. Binns, a former student of mine, aided by his wife, conducted the pilot study on which Table II is based.
4. *Democrat & Chronicle*, Rochester, New York, May 26, 1970, p. 8B.
5. F.B. Gilbreth, *Bricklaying System*, M.C. Clark, 1909.
6. Lillian M. Gilbreth, Orpha Mae Thomas, and Eleanor Clymer, *Management in the Home*, New York, Dodd, Mead & Company, 1955, pp. 65-66.

Chapter 6

VENTURE INTO THE WORLD OUTSIDE

*Our conscience has been reawakened
to the contribution individuals can
make not merely by being good parents but also by using their individual
gifts.*

MARGARET MEAD
Epilogue to *American Women*[1]

The Stage Has Been Set

MANY women who have followed the road to self-development
described so far will have decided to explore opportunities for self-
fulfillment outside the home. Once this self-knowledge has been
acquired and more efficient methods of home management have
been implemented, you are ready to venture into the world outside.
Education, business, government, and volunteer work now offer
more attractive alternatives to women than existed in the past.

Colleges and universities have developed new programs to meet
the needs of the homemaker-student. Many more will follow in
their path. Most schools are facing financial pressures today and
will face them for at least the next decade. Tuition dollars are
welcomed, whether they come from an eighteen-year-old fresh-
man or a forty-five-year-old mother of five children. Aside from
this financial fact of life, more colleges are becoming more mindful
of the needs of the community.

Employers are being made more aware of the importance of better
opportunities for women. Feminists and various consumer groups
have created pressure in this direction. Federal legislation now
makes it illegal to discriminate against women. You may have a
smaller chance than your husband of becoming a corporate execu-

tive, but rewarding positions in business, government, and education can still be found. Looking at the positive side of the picture, 50 percent of the managers in United States department stores, 25 percent of managers in insurance companies, and 11 percent of the officers in banks are women.[2] Many of these managerial positions are at the bottom rung of management; nevertheless the female assistant vice president of loans receives more of self-fulfillment than her counterpart who sits at home and complains about anti-female discrimination.

Volunteer groups are now finding more significant causes to champion, such as environmental pollution and racial discrimination, and even female discrimination problems. Volunteer work must still be approached with caution if you are looking for self-fulfillment, but the outlook is becoming brighter.

This chapter provides some suggestions for finding educational programs, paid jobs, or volunteer work that will help you achieve a more integrated and fulfilling life.

Return to Formal Schooling

Return to formal schooling represents the first step toward self-fulfillment for many women. Education, to small numbers of women, will be an end in itself. Many of their needs for a fuller life can be met through the process of taking courses. Patricia Jackson, a homemaker, expresses it this way:

> Yeah, some of my friends and neighbors think I'm just a perpetual student. Well I am, and for very good reasons that most people can't understand. Learning is fun and also very exciting. To me it's a lot more worthwhile than getting a job or taking up some hobby. I guess you could say that I just want intellectual stimulation. But at least I know what I want.

Formal schooling for most women represents a means to an end; schooling will help them reach some other goal that is important in strengthening their self-image. Thus the housewife who decides that many of her needs for recognition and status can be met through personnel work chooses to take courses in human relations and personnel psychology. Ideally these courses will enhance her credentials for personnel work and her knowledge that can be applied to the job.

Completion of the Self-Knowledge Questionnaire and career counseling provide valuable information for selecting an educational program suitable to your interests. However, even after all this information is gathered, three vital questions remain:

1. Why (for what purposes) am I going to school?
2. Where (at what institution) should I attend school?
3. Which courses should I take?

Why Return to School?

Your chances for a meaningful educational experience will increase if you understand your motives for attending school. The broadest purpose for your returning to school is to become a woman in transition. Formal schooling can be a vehicle to bring you one step closer to self-realization. However noble this motive, it may be too abstract to provide you with the motivational thrust necessary to help you drive to class in a snow storm or study economic theory on a warm spring afternoon. Sometimes you need a specific, tangible purpose for attending school.

Purposes of formal schooling can be divided roughly into education and training. Education is intended to provide you with enrichment, stimulation, and intellectual broadening. Education is a long-term and hopefully lifetime process. You might decide that intellectual stimulation is your goal. Toward this end seek out courses that provide good fundamental knowledge. Don't worry about applying this knowledge tomorrow; that is not the purpose of education. Political science, history, art appreciation, genetics, cybernetics, medieval literature, and the sociology of religion are but a few examples of educational courses. They provide you intellectual stimulation but not a set of skills that you can apply to the home or job situation tomorrow.

Training, in contrast to education, is designed to teach you tangible skills that you can put into practice. Suppose you decide that selling real estate would provide you the personal rewards you are seeking. Careful review of real estate licensing requirements in your state indicates that you need a broker's license. More education would be worthwhile, but would only be remotely related to your immediate goal. Attend a training program in real estate selling, whether it is offered by a university or a certified home study course. You need to acquire some specific skills in a hurry. Education cannot be rushed, but training can. Later on take a course in macroeconomics to increase your depth of understanding about forces shaping the price of real estate. However, you do not need this knowledge right now.

Women with preschool children often lament, "Why should I get involved with taking courses now? There is no place for me to apply the knowledge that I might pick up. My friends and husband aren't particularly interested in hearing me talk about my school work." Such a rationalization against taking courses overlooks an important purpose of training and education for women at home—the prevention of obsolescence. Homemakers are faced with the threat of becoming obsolete in terms of basic skills and knowledge required to cope effectively with the world outside the home. You might judge the degree to which you are becoming occupationally obsolete by answering these basic questions:

1. When was the last time I wrote a formal letter or memo?
2. When was the last time I tried to sell an idea or plan to a group of people?
3. How long has it been since I had to gather up some factual information and make a decision based upon the information I found?
4. How good are my arithmetic skills?
5. How confident am I in my ability to work on an equal level with a male adult?
6. Would I have less to offer a prospective employer now than I had when I was twenty-one?

Successful performance in course work has the built-in fringe benefit of keeping a woman confident of her mental ability. In turn, this positive attitude helps combat obsolescence.

Attendance at a college, university, or extension center also fulfills an important social purpose. Many women who suffer the housewife syndrome are unabashedly looking for new adult companionship. Recognizing this purpose will help direct you toward the right kind of courses, and the right kind of educational institution to meet your needs. Here is an honest statement from a twenty-eight-year-old housewife:

> The best part about returning to school has been the people I've met. The class discussions are good, too. I'm not all that interested in memorizing a bunch of facts. That course in child psychology I took was mostly a rap session and I liked it real well. The men and women in the class were fine people.

In short, if your motive in returning to school is social, don't overload yourself on the intellectual side. Take courses that emphasize group interaction, not the acquisition of factual information. Find out where the type of people—male or female—that you prefer are more likely to be found. You might even decide that social clubs are better suited to your purpose than educational institutions.

Where to Attend School?

To a large extent, where you attend school depends upon *why* you are attending school, as alluded to in our last example. Housewives returning to school are usually apprehensive about both the rigidity of admission standards and the prospects of being unwelcome on the campus. Some of these apprehensions can be cast aside. Today many colleges and universities are designing programs specifically to suit the needs of homemakers.

Universities are composed of different schools, each with different purposes and different admission standards. Admission to the graduate school of arts and sciences at a select university may be difficult if you have a fifteen-year-old bachelor's degree (with a C average) from a state teachers' college. Perhaps all you are seeking at this time is three refresher courses to qualify for teacher certification. Another school within the university may be able to accommodate you.

Most universities contain a college of continuing education, university school, night school, or adult extension center. These schools usually have liberal (or wide open) admission standards, and welcome students of all ages and educational backgrounds. It is possible to pursue degree or nondegree programs at these schools.

Colleges of continuing education offer courses that appeal to people with a wide variety of interests and academic ability. Here is a sampling of the courses listed in the catalogue of one college of continuing education: Report Writing, Oral Communications, Western

Civilization, Introduction to Drama, Analytic Geometry and Calculus, Microelectronics, Marketing Motivation and Persuasion.

Where you attend school will also be influenced by the importance you attach to a formal degree. Obtaining a degree involves more hurdles than pursuing a nondegree program. Complexities such as transfers of credit and course prerequisites are more often associated with the former. Nondegree programs are useful for a variety of purposes. The following goals could be met by education or training programs that are classified as nondegree:

> I'm interested mostly in improving my mind.
>
> What is important to me is to develop some basic skills that I could offer to an employer.
>
> I've been dabbling around in photography for long enough. I need some more depth knowledge in that field.
>
> It's about time I followed somebody else's orders again. As a housewife I set my own standards for everything. A college course would teach me how to do assignments for somebody else.

However, the importance of a formal degree for many purposes cannot be dismissed. Some women (as well as men) need the external push of working toward something tangible. Here are some goals that can be reached only by obtaining a degree:

> I need to accomplish something that my children and husband would be proud of. I need to prove to myself and others that I can follow through on something important.
>
> I've done some substitute teaching, but it's not quite enough for me. I want to become a specialist in counseling and guidance.
>
> Taking care of the family finances has always been fun for me. I've been the treasurer in every group I've belonged to. I know I'd make a good CPA, and I'm going to prove it.
>
> My first love is microbiology. I had terrific marks in college in that subject. With a master's degree in microbiology there would be no holding me back in the laboratory.

Traditional degree programs are offered by all accredited colleges and universities. Entrance requirements, prerequisites, and residence requirements are less flexible than in schools of continuing education. Full-time attendance for one or two years is usually required to obtain a degree. Students in the traditional degree program are mostly in the seventeen- to twenty-two-year-old age bracket. Housewives returning to school sometimes question their ability to establish rapport with young adults. These feelings are usually overcome after a brief period of orientation. Said a thirty-nine-year-old mother of two:

> The kids (college students) have been great to me. They treat me as an equal except that they are always willing to give me a hand. One girl young enough to be my daughter has been tutoring me in statistics. She's a whiz, and I couldn't make it without her help.

Within a given university or college, the traditional four-year school usually demands higher academic performance from students than do colleges of continuing education or extension centers. Degrees virtually identical in value, however, can usually be obtained from both schools.

Community colleges, like schools of continuing education, adhere to a democratic philosophy of education. Sometimes called junior or city colleges, these schools usually only require that you be a resident of the community in order to qualify for admission. Two-year degrees, called associate degrees, are their specialty. An associate's degree offers the psychological advantage of being a more attainable goal than a four- or five-year degree. Once the associate's degree is earned, it can then be cashed in as half the requirement for a bachelor's degree at a large number of four-year colleges.

Community colleges offer liberal arts, business, and technical programs. Women interested in such occupations as laboratory technician, computer programmer, or executive secretary find these schools quite satisfactory.

Extension centers are one method of bringing formal education closer to your home. These centers are sometimes more flexible about residency requirements and the length of time in which you are allowed to work on one degree. It is not unusual for a woman to work eight years toward a bachelor's degree at an extension center. Extension center students, on the average, are older than undergraduates in on-campus programs. Many work full-time outside the home, and many are homemakers. Students have commented that they enjoy extension school (and other night schools) because all the students are "serious."

Private schools designed to train you in specific occupational skills may represent the solution of choice for many women. Suppose one woman concluded that beauty salon management would be a worthwhile goal for her to pursue. She would achieve the trade knowledge considered necessary for this field more directly through a private school than through a public college or technical institute.

Correspondence school, educational television, and other forms of self-study may be educationally sound but have some distinct limitations for the woman seeking to strengthen her self-image. Exchanging ideas with other students, making comments in class, and listening to the spontaneous comments of instructors contributes heavily to your education and training. These informal benefits are lost when all of your program is self-study.

Where you attend school, providing you can find the courses you need, may be less important than you realize. Radcliffe may have more status as an institution of higher learning than your local community college, but both institutions have one thing in common: they only play a small part in your formal education. Most of the benefit of any kind of educational or training experience is directly proportional to effort you are willing to expend. If self-fulfillment is your goal you must assume an active, almost tenacious attitude about study.

What about the calibre of professors? Don't better-known schools have better-known (and therefore more effective) professors? Paradoxically, sometimes lesser-known schools have instructors who are more interested in students. This is not an absolute generalization, but it holds some merit. Instructors who are emotionally involved in their own writings or research sometimes spend too much time talking about their own ideas. Major accomplishments in their field might go unmentioned while they devote lecture time to discussing their personal work.

Which Courses Should I Take?

The safest advice here is to consult with an educational counselor or advisor furnished by the school. He or she should be able to assist you in taking courses that are consistent with the plans you have developed for yourself. Following are five suggestions for selecting courses that will ease your transition back to school:

1. Upon returning to school choose a course that appears relatively easy. Courses whereby the process of living (experience) gives you some slight edge fall into the "easy" category. For example, a course

in contemporary issues gives you a chance to use some of the knowledge you have accumulated over the years. In contrast, most women have no experience that can be applied directly to a course in computer programming. Taking a course in the adult education division of a high school is sometimes a good warm-up for returning to college, either at the graduate or undergraduate level.

2. After having flexed your intellectual muscles and acquired some systematic study habits, the best educational strategy for most people is to take courses which stretch but do not frustrate you. Every student should take some difficult courses, but too many of these will lower your self-confidence. Remember, one of the purposes of returning to school is to strengthen your self-image.

> Carol Baldwin and Myra Arnold both expressed disappointment after having completed one year of course work. Carol was frustrated because she received A's in two courses but felt no intellectual growth taking place. Her courses were Gourmet Cooking and Current Events. Myra was frustrated because she received two D's, and questioned whether or not she should continue with her educational program. Her courses were Introduction to Thermodynamics and Physiological Psychology.

Experience in taking courses is necessary to accurately select courses that will be at an appropriate level of difficulty for you. Discussions with an educational counselor at your school should be helpful in making sound course selections.

3. Attempt to take courses that fit into some kind of master plan for self-fulfillment. The time at which a particular course meets should be a secondary consideration to its content and its relevance to your overall goals. (One woman selected a hodgepodge of courses for herself, simply because she tried to have them coincide with her husband's bowling schedule.) Many courses are inherently stimulating, but if you have some outside purpose for taking them, they seem even more worthwhile.

4. Search for some courses that involve class discussion or group interaction. Intellectual passivity is one of the major problems facing homemakers. Courses that encourage students to confront and challenge each other's ideas provide an outstanding opportunity for intellectual and emotional growth. Obviously, courses in the behavioral and social sciences and the humanities provide more opportunity for

discussion than do courses in the physical sciences.

5. Use college catalogues as guidelines, not rigid rules. Many of the procedures and regulations described within catalogues sound much different when interpreted by a college advisor or professor. Frequently special permission can be granted to overcome a catalogue requirement.

> Louise Eldridge, a fifty-year-old housewife, had a lifelong phobia about swimming. One requirement for graduating from the college where Louise was a part-time student was to pass a water safety test. Special allowances were made in her situation by an understanding member of the administration.

Conducting Your Job Campaign

Education for many women is one important stepping-stone on the path back to work. Next comes the demanding chore of conducting a job campaign.[3]

> Susan Roman is a homemaker with three children. Her youngest child has just entered the first grade. Susan feels that only the world of work will provide her with the feeling of recognition and accomplishment she needs to strengthen her self-image and avoid the housewife syndrome. Before she was married, Sue received a bachelor's degree in history and was qualified to teach at the high school level. To strengthen her credentials for a position in business, Sue recently acquired a bachelor's degree in business administration. (Because Sue is a college graduate, she was only required to take several courses to obtain this degree.) She now feels ready to find a job. Sue will not be alone; 50 percent of women with all their children in school are part of the labor force, either by choice or economic necessity.

Step one in launching a job campaign is to prepare a resume. Most homemakers dislike preparing a resume, because most of what they have accomplished in recent years (such as raising a family) is not applicable to business. Reluctance, however, is no excuse. A resume is important for several reasons: (1) It helps you crystallize your thinking about your potential contribution to an employer. (Most of the information you need for a resume is already contained in the Self-Knowledge Questionnaire.) (2) Employers, particularly personnel specialists, expect applicants for higher-level jobs to have prepared a resume. There is a minor element of "upmanship" in having a resume, but every detail counts when you are seeking employment.

(3) Self-discipline, attention to detail, and organization of your thoughts is required in preparing a resume. These are skills you will need to succeed in any organization. You might as well get started practicing them. After several tries, here is the resume Sue Roman wrote.

RESUME

Susan T. Roman   Age 32
62 Benedict Drive   Married, three children
Milwaukee, Wisconsin 53215   Phone: 244-4048

Job Objective

Administrative Assistant to executive, or Personnel Specialist

Job Experience

1965–   Taught high school History and Government on substitute basis in local high schools; approximately one day per month during school year.

1963–1964 Shamrock Agency, Chicago, Illinois
           Employment agency interviewer; interviewed job applicants; conferred with local employers about job vacancies and the qualifications of applicants. Considerable telephone canvassing required. Left because of advanced stages of pregnancy.

1962–1963 Systems Mutual Insurance Company, Chicago, Illinois
           Personnel specialist; assisted in the hiring and placement of clerical and secretarial personnel. Left for higher-paying position and more responsibility.

Volunteer Work Experience

1969–1970 Headed committee to study drug control in local junior high school. Group met ten times and received recognition from local government.

1968–   Assist in door-to-door Community Chest fund raising every spring. Have been neighborhood coordinator for three years.

1966–1969 Editor for Newcomer's Newsletter. Every two months collected pertinent information and put it together in proper format. Each issue also contained a small editorial that I personally put together.

Formal Education

           Bryant Institute of Technology
           Received B.S. degree in Business Administration in 1972. Courses emphasized practical application of knowledge.

University of Wisconsin
Received B.A. degree in History in 1962. My extracurricular activities were college newspaper reporter, cheerleader.
West Milwaukee High School
Academic diploma in 1958. Cheerleader, I was president of English Club, and member of Student Council.

Skills

Experienced interviewer; able to express self well in speaking and writing; relate well to people; accurate with numbers and record keeping.

Effective resumes are straightforward, factual presentations of experience and accomplishments. Exact rules about how to prepare a resume are usually unreliable. Two extremes, however, should be avoided. One unacceptable extreme is to prepare a flamboyant, overdrawn presentation of your credentials and accomplishments. Thus, a woman who had worked in the registrar's office of a university might note on her resume:

1960-1970 New York University
During my tenure with NYU, enrollment doubled, and large numbers of well-known scholars were brought to the university.

Her statement may be factually correct, but this woman's contribution to the growth of the school was probably smaller than she inferred in the resume.

Another extreme to avoid is chatty, informal statements about trivial matters. Observe the trivial, chatty nature of this resume entry:

Hobbies I have always enjoyed reading as a way of stimulating my mind. Next to reading, my favorite hobby is playing with my three wonderful children, Mike, Randy, and Sally. Gardening, particularly roses and azaleas, is another favorite of mine. I guess you could say people are another hobby of mine. I like people and am looking for a job working with them.

Despite its widespread practice it is questionable whether hobbies and interests should be mentioned in a resume. The purpose of a resume is to present an overview of your background. More detailed information can be presented during the employment interview.

Finding a Job

Once your resume is prepared you are ready to look for a job. Recommendation one is to use the "overkill" in searching for a suitable position. Forty, fifty, or sixty contacts could be required before you make the right connection between your qualifications and the need for such qualifications.

Job contacts come from many sources. First you should ask your husband, friends, and acquaintances about any position opening they may have heard about that coincides with your job objective. The person speaking on your behalf may in turn be referred to a third party who is aware of a job vacancy. Other people, of course, cannot be pushed into exploring job opportunities for you. Many people are hesitant to recommend friends to employers as prospective employees. Should you be hired and fail or shortly quit, it reflects negatively on their judgment about people.

Classified advertisements in newspapers and trade magazines are a key source of job openings. Each ad strongly suggests that an employer is actually looking to fill a specific position. (There are some instances when employers list openings with no intent to hire, just to maintain a steady stream of job applicants.) Each letter sent to a prospective employer should be accompanied by a resume. Aside from carefully summarizing your suitability for the job, they have a political advantage. Many of your competitors for these positions will not have taken the trouble to prepare a resume.

Don't be chagrined when your first response to a classified advertisement doesn't yield a quick reply. Attractive-sounding jobs, even in a tight labor market, gather in large numbers of applicants. Job hunting is an imprecise process.

Employment agencies, both private and governmental, represent another standard approach to finding a job. Fees charged by such agencies must be considered in relation to the contribution suitable employment can make to your self image. Employment agencies vary in their ability to find you a job that dovetails your interests and abilities. However, as in any other business, agencies need satisfied customers.

Agency personnel sometime make useful suggestions to job candidates. One woman was looking for a position in which she could apply her earlier background in teaching outside of a school setting. The employment counselor suggested a human relations training position within a telephone company, which proved to be an excellent fit.

Writing directly to organizations where you would like to work sometimes pays dividends. First call the organization to learn the personnel director's name. Letters addressed to a specific individual and typed—not reproduced—attract more favorable attention than do mass-produced "Dear Sir" letters. Accompanying a typed letter with a reproduced resume is considered standard business practice. Probably 90 percent of unsolicited resumes pass quickly over someone's desk into the wastebasket, but you might fall into the fortunate 10 percent. Exceptions occur primarily when there is an opening somewhere in the company that fits your particular background. Remember that even though the probability of finding a job by this method might be dismally low, you are only looking for one job.

Maintain a flexible attitude in conducting your job search. Susan Roman was looking for an administrative assistant or personnel specialist position. "Administrative Assistant" sounds quite specific, but it could include any position from a White House aide to a high-level secretary. Your goals should focus on the type of work you want, but remember the same type of work can be found in many different positions. Should working with numbers and figures be your preference you can satisfy these interests in such diverse jobs as wage and salary analyst, bookkeeper, sales order specialist, or tax assistant.

Here is how flexibility paid dividends for Susan. She learned through personal contacts that the personnel department of a large company was creating the position of "Tuition Refund Coordinator." On the surface this job does not sound loaded with opportunities for self-fulfillment. Susan recognized some of its hidden value after discussion with the prospective boss. She would be responsible for listening to the case of each person in the company who wished to apply for tuition refund. Those cases that seemed to meet company policy would be referred to her boss for final approval. In this job Susan would interview people about pleasant matters, keep records, interpret company policy, and make some decisions of her own. In one position Susan achieved both job objectives: administrative assistant and personnel specialist. Note that she had never heard the term "Tuition Refund Coordinator" before speaking to this company.

Your Job Interview

Women who have achieved success in the early stages of their job campaign will be granted a job interview, either with their prospective boss or a representative of the personnel department. Most women are apprehensive about this interview. All but the most inveterate job hoppers feel some anxiety when faced with the prospect of a job interview. Some degree of tension is therefore expected and normal. Following are some general hints that should increase your chances of having a successful interview. Your judgment is probably better than mine about such matters as the proper length of skirt to wear to an interview.

First, do your homework. Be familiar with all pertinent details of your background and experiences, including the names of references. Even take the time to memorize your social security number. Preparing your resume should have brought you up to date about your background. Knowledge of the major activities or business of your prospective employer is also helpful. Job applicants unfamiliar with the nature of the job they are applying for bring unfavorable attention to themselves. For example, if you apply for a public relations specialist position, first skim through a book about public relations.

Second, have reasons to justify your plans. By now you should have carefully thought through why you are seeking a job and why you want the particular job for which you are being interviewed. Positive reasons for seeking a position are more impressive than negative reasons. Observe the different impact created by these two women:

> *Casework Supervisor:* Why do you want to be a caseworker?
>
> *Woman No. 1:* Staying home taking care of children has gotten to me. I just about can't stand it anymore. A job is what I need to ward off the housewife syndrome.
>
> *Woman No. 2:* This isn't a new interest with me. I had planned to get involved in a helping profession once my children no longer required my full-time attention.

Third, focus on important aspects of the job, not upon its trivial elements. Women (and men) unfamiliar with being interviewed often relieve their anxiety by asking questions about noncontroversial topics such as working hours, frequency of getting paid, and cafeteria facilities. Perceptive interviewers—particularly if you are applying for a higher-level job—will think you are narrow in outlook if you dwell on such matters. Remember, the major reason you are seeking employment at this time is to find more accomplishment. How often you get paid and the length of lunch breaks show little relationship to accomplishment.

Fourth, don't worry about hidden meanings behind questions. Few interview questions are as revealing as you think. Often the person conducting the interview does not know the rationale behind the questions he or she asks. Unless your responses are grossly atypical, much of what you say goes unrecorded. Job interviewers frequently ask you to name your biggest weakness. Comments such as "bad temper," "poor with numbers," "a little tardy sometimes," "keep my feelings inside," "hate to hurt others' feelings," "get impatient," and "get tired at the end of the day" are certainly within the normal range. Comments such as "My last boss said I was a castrating female" or "I can't be trusted with company money" would make a personnel man take notice. In general, the best defense against all questions is a straightforward presentation of the facts as you know them. You are expected to place yourself in a favorable light but deliberate falsification of information is an employment no-no!

Fifth, allow the interviewer to talk. Many employment interviewers are less than expert interviewers. One employment specialist I know uses much of the job interview to tell applicants about his accomplishments in life. The mature person can laugh at this situation. Also, you will benefit from listening to the interviewer talk. You will be rated as "skillful in communications" and "insightful." Exercise your intuition, however, to determine when the interviewer is through talking and wants you to carry the conversation.

Success Factors for Women

Managers of the future will probably show less prejudice against females than their older, more traditional counterparts, but you have to cope with the world as it exists today. Most hints on how to be successful in organizational life apply to both men and women. Competence and hard work combined with good luck is still the secret to success in all but the most political and nepotistic organizations. Following are five suggestions that the perceptive and success-oriented woman should ponder as she competes with others in organizational life.

Be Unequal Competition. Antifemale prejudice dictates that you have to outperform males in order to receive identical treatment. In the words of Edith Grimm, a high-ranking female executive, the woman who succeeds in business must "look like a girl, act like a lady, think like a man, and work like a dog."[4]

Handle Male Insecurities. Many men are threatened by women equally competent or more competent than themselves. Few men, for example, would choose to work for a woman. Should your insight into people tell you that your boss (and his boss) feel uneasy about having a competent female performing work similar to theirs, take this advice offered by Alice S. Rossi, a prominent sociologist: ". . . Ask a man's opinions about your ideas, show gratitude for his help, make your points as questions, listen with respect and interest to his ideas, and in this way you may be accepted. Even the most insecure type of male will not resent your achievements if you are quiet about them."[5]

Soft-Pedal Feminism. If you are ambitious and interested in genuine accomplishment, you will want to get promoted and receive other rewards because of your talent, not your sex. Women who demand to be promoted because they are female, not because they merit the promotion, are distorting the purpose of feminism. This is a subtle but an important difference. Women's liberation can only lay the groundwork for your receiving equal treatment. If you are seeking self-fulfillment, it would be self-defeating for you to be promoted on the basis of sex rather than merit.

Carefully Balance Work and Family Demands. Women who find employment outside the home all too often double their work load. Poor performance in both the homemaker and career roles can be the net result. Positive, constructive approaches have to be taken to prevent this problem. Explicit arrangements with husbands and older children should be made with regard to homemaking chores. Subcontracting homemaking chores to domestic help or professional housecleaners is often the solution of choice. Suitable day care arrangements for young children are essential for your peace of mind. Women preoccupied with concerns about the welfare of their children have difficulty focusing their attention on job matters. Average or less than average job performance is frequently the result. Exceptions to this rule come only in the case of mothers who experience no guilt about neglecting the well-being of their children.

Emotionalism Can Hurt You. People—women are as guilty as men—expect emotionalism to be the Achilles' heel of women at work. One male company president concisely sums up all the stereotyped notions about female emotionalism on the job: ". . . women are incurably addicted to jealousy, favoritism, and decisions based on emotion or intuition rather than facts or reason."

Despite the flaws in this generalization it contains one element of psychological truth. Women in general are more emotionally expressive than men. However, professional and executive women, similar to their male counterparts, display a healthy degree of emotional reserve; they are "cool." People wait for career women to demonstrate emotionalism to prove that their stereotypes about women are correct. Why add more fuel to their distortions about women? In the words of Robert Townsend, author of *Up the Organization,* "You're entitled to burst into tears once per career. More than that, and your self-control (an executive quality not to be dismissed lightly) is in doubt."[6]

Volunteer with Caution

Volunteer work is another alternative facing the woman in transition. Such work has its advantages: (a) Assignments can be scheduled around your family obligations. (b) Educational requirements are liberal. (c) Jobs are plentiful. (d) Volunteer work relieves guilt feelings you might have about not making a contribution to society. Most communities have a volunteer bureau which acts as a clearinghouse to match up your interests and available opportunities. They represent a good starting point for exploring the volunteer work possibilities for yourself.

Despite these advantages of volunteer work, you must exercise caution before choosing volunteer work as an approach to self-fulfillment. Many women have experienced more frustration than satisfaction in volunteer work. Following is an overview of three key sources of frustration in volunteer work.

Good Jobs Go to Professionals. Women usually seek out volunteer work to find activities of greater intellectual challenge than homemaking. Discouragingly, initial assignments in such work are usually menial in nature. One woman eager to provide a useful service to the community joined the volunteer wing of her church. Her first assignment was to arrange a baked goods sale.

> Never again will I get involved in a mess like that. Most of the women who said they would bake a cake didn't. I wound up baking twelve cakes and washing about one hundred plates. I chose volunteer work to get away from the kitchen, not to become pantry help.

Envelope stuffing is another assignment frequently offered to the neophyte volunteer. Choicer assignments usually go to full-time professional-level help or to women with high seniority in the organization. One woman enlisted the services of two preadolescent girls to help her with mailings. In this way she organized getting the low-level clerical tasks accomplished rather than doing them herself.

Many Volunteer Groups Lack Real Purpose. It is not uncommon for volunteer organizations to be without a specific, meaningful purpose. Some volunteer groups exist merely to give members an excuse to socialize with one another. For example, one volunteer group hoped to culturally enrich inner city members. They attempted to organize museum trips for inner city residents, only to find that this function was already being performed by the public schools. Yet they continued to hold meetings. Unless your volunteer group has a meaningful purpose, you cannot hope to derive a feeling of satisfaction and accomplishment from attending its meetings. If you belong to a purposeless group, helping it find a purpose could be a source of personal satisfaction. Causes such as pollution control and population control have become more popular in recent years, thus providing new outlets for the energies of many volunteer groups.

Status Outweighs Talent. In wealthier, more established communities there is often a waiting list to obtain choice volunteer assignments. When these assignments become available, they are frequently doled out according to the status of your family background or the occupation of your husband. In one hospital only doctors' wives can obtain key volunteer assignments. The woman's club at one university reserves officerships for the wives of husbands with Ph.D.'s and who work in high-prestige departments. Women who choose volunteer work to achieve some status of their own—independent of their husbands'—will be defeating their own purposes by belonging to such groups.

Despite these reservations about volunteer work as a vehicle for self-fulfillment, its potential contribution to your self-development should not be dismissed. Finding a volunteer assignment that matches your capability and provides you personal rewards is difficult but not impossible. After a careful search one woman found a volunteer position as a tour guide in an art museum. This assignment dictated that she study art and also helped develop her skills in dealing with people.

Bring the Outside World Inside

Family responsibilities prohibit attendance at school, full- or part-time work, or even volunteer work for some women. Another option still exists which can at least get you started on the path toward broader responsibilities in life than homemaking. Bring a small piece of the outside world into your home in the form of home study courses, or modest types of work. Besides, if you have enough creativity and talent, working inside your home is the solution of choice. Writers, artists, and sculptors frequently *choose* to work out of their homes. Work conducted in the home lacks the important advantage of contact with adults, but at least you will be developing skills that can later be used in outside employment.

What are some of these "outside-inside" jobs? Those requiring creative ability include writing greeting card messages, selling product ideas (a homemaker-inventor, for example, thought of the disposable paperboard serving tray), and restoring and repairing art objects. Less creative ability is required for assignments such as telephone soliciting, running a baby-sitting registry service, or working for a newspaper and magazine clipping service. Finding the right inside job for yourself will require a lot of digging.[7]

You Have to Expect Some Frustrations

Homemakers tend to overglamorize the role of the career woman. In truth, career women encounter many frustrations in their work. Even if you have an above average job, you will have to cope with picayune political battles, hurt feelings, and other forms of immature behavior. Said one woman manager in an insurance company:

I used to think my children were immature. Now I know better. These girls fight about everything. One girl wants to be transferred to a department where there is a better chance to meet a man. Another quit her job for three dollars more per week. I almost gave up my job when one of the girls accused me of playing favorites because I allowed another girl time off with pay to go on her honeymoon.

On balance, the world outside contains more opportunities for self-fulfillment than can be found in a full-time homemaking role for most women. This does not mean that every woman finds self-fulfillment in work. Most jobs, even executive-level and professional positions, do not provide a steady stream of emotional and intellectual stimulation. Furthermore, the more exciting and challenging jobs in any organization have to be earned. An enriched and more fulfilling life is a worthwhile goal to pursue, but there are many built-in frustrations along the way. Don't surrender your new life plans when you encounter your first frustration.

NOTES

1. Margaret Mead, Epilogue to *American Women*, New York, Charles Scribner's Sons, 1965, p. 202, quoted in Gladys E. Harbeson, *Choice and Challenge for the American Woman*, Cambridge, Mass., Schenkman Publishing Company, 1967.
2. American Management Association brochure describing conference entitled "Women Managers & Administrators: Management Training & Development," April 28-30, 1971, New York City.
3. Many of the general ideas here are based on material in Nanette E. Scofield and Betty Klarman, *So You Want to Go Back to Work*, New York, Random House, 1968.
4. "For Women, a Difficult Climb to the Top," *Business Week*, Aug. 2, 1969, p. 46.
5. Alice S. Rossi, "Job Discrimination and What Women Can Do About It," *Atlantic*, 225:100, Mar. 1970.
6. Quoted in *Democrat & Chronicle*, Rochester, New York, April 18, 1971, p. 8E.
7. For useful ideas on this topic, see Barbara Creaturo, "27 Jobs for Bored Young Housewives," *Cosmopolitan*, Dec. 1969, pp. 60-68.

Chapter 7

THE AFFAIR AS A SOLUTION

Do not adultery commit; advantage rarely comes of it.

ARTHUR HUGH CLOUGH
The Latest Decalogue

The psychology of adultery has been falsified by conventional morals, which assume, in monogamous countries, that attraction to one person cannot coexist with a serious affection for another. Everybody knows that this is untrue.

BERTRAND RUSSELL
Marriage and Morals

Why Do Wives Have Affairs?

SEXOLOGISTS, marriage counselors, psychiatrists, psychologists, and newspaper columnists, among others, have made frequent attempts at analyzing the reasons why many homemakers find sexual outlets with people other than their husbands. Sifting through a multitude of explanations, five major reasons married women have affairs are these: (1) Affairs hold some promise of relief from boredom, monotony, and loneliness. (2) Affairs are frequently a reaction to marital difficulties both sexual and nonsexual in origin. (3) Hostility and revenge directed toward the husband underlie many situations of infidelity. (4) The quest for self-esteem, approval, and recognition directs some women toward relationships with men other than their spouses. (5) The desire to become part of the new morality prompts some women to have affairs.

Feelings of boredom, monotony, and loneliness are all well-

116

documented symptoms of the housewife syndrome. Few full-time homemakers are exempt from at least occasional pangs of these emotions. Loneliness can be felt even by the woman surrounded by children and in frequent contact with her spouse; not only the alone are lonely. An important distinction can be drawn between loneliness and aloneness. Women whose husbands do not care about them in a deep and meaningful way experience loneliness even if their husbands spend substantial time at home.

Loneliness, boredom, and monotony are intertwined. Emotional loneliness predisposes people toward becoming bored with their daily activities, while being bored creates a desire for a more intense emotional relationship with another person. For many homemakers, an extra-marital affair holds considerable promise of relief from these feelings. Men in search of female companionship yet who fear the entanglement that might stem from relationships with single, divorced, or widowed women often direct their attention toward married women. Men whose occupation places them in daytime contact with housewives are alleged to lead diverse and exciting social lives. An implicit fringe benefit for athletic instructors and waiters at resorts and country clubs is the opportunity to meet women in search of extramarital affairs.

One woman describes the reasons for her affair:

> Why did I have this affair? I think you should ask me why not. I was very bored and lonely at the time. This has been a down period in my life. My husband talks only about business and our daughter. This man came along and really listened to me. I think he liked me as a person, even though we only saw each other a few times. I know that I will see him again sometime even though he lives in another city. Spending time with him made my life less boring.

Extramarital affairs, at a minimum, are good short-range antidotes to boredom, monotony, and loneliness. Sexual activity with a partner of positive social stimulus value (in your eyes) is intrinsically interesting, nonrepetitious, and nonlonely. Longer-range disadvantages, such as potential guilt feelings and magnification of marital problems, will be alluded to later.

Adultery is more frequently a symptom than a cause of marital problems. The comment, "My marriage has gone bad ever since my wife started seeing another man," might more appropriately be changed to "My wife started seeing another man ever since our marriage went bad." Sexual incompatibility between husband and wife is the precipitating factor for many women to find another sex partner without giving up the security of marriage. Women who become disinterested in sex with their spouse are not necessarily disinterested in sex with another man. Sexual problems in turn may be a reflection of general incompatibility between husband and wife. One woman with a successful experience in psychotherapy provides the following insight:

> My problems with my husband began when I gained strength as a person. Once I found myself and was no longer that helpless, dependent, frightened little bird, he could no longer love me. It began with a lot of petty little arguments. Then he lost interest in our sex life together. His sickness only showed up when I got well.

Adultery sometimes represents a convenient escape from squarely confronting marital problems. Both partners may recognize that the other is having an affair but each rationalizes that this is a preferable alternative to divorce or separation. Women thus may use an affair to preserve the remnants of their marriage. Without recourse to an emotional and physical outlet other than an incompatible spouse, marriage would be an untenable life situation. The affair provides just enough satisfaction to keep life in a state of equilibrium. Confrontation with the significant issues eroding away at the structure of their marriage is thus avoided.

Hostility and revenge directed at the husband in retaliation for his behavior constitute another female motive for adultery. Husbands may precipitate these kinds of reactions in women because of both actions and attitudes. Actions evoking the reactions of hostility and revenge include extramarital affairs, attention directed toward other women, or physical abuse. Abiding by the Hammurabi code of human conduct the woman feels that "you've had your fling, now it's my turn." Sometimes indiscretions of the other spouse are used as justification for a long-desired affair. Unconsciously one spouse might even facilitate the other's having an affair in order to relieve guilt feelings about a contemplated affair. Observe the underlying motivation of the woman who requested the following favor of her husband:

> Doris is quite distressed these days. She is having all sorts of problems with her husband and I don't think I can help her. She has always admired and respected you. I'm not the jealous type and Doris is my friend. Why don't you take her to lunch sometime next week?

This plan, however naive and transparent it appears in presentation, accomplished its purpose. The obliging husband did have an affair with Doris, his wife did hear about it through a third party, and she did then justify to her own satisfaction an affair with another man.

Retaliation, revenge, and hostility directed toward the husband may also be manifested in an affair when the husband's transgressions lie outside the sexual sphere. Women sometimes pursue adultery because of the husband's noninvolvement in their relationship. The "lazy husband syndrome" is a situation whereby the husband is uninvolved with his job, wife, and children. One woman married to a man so afflicted said to her lover, "Don't be too concerned about him finding out about us. I don't think he even cares. He would only object if our getting together meant that he had to take care of the kids during the football game."

Successful husbands may also predispose their wives toward extramarital affairs by preoccupying themselves with work and paying only surface attention to the emotional needs of their wives in the process. Sexual intercourse with another person, according to the wives of some successful husbands, is no more an act of unfaithfulness than is total preoccupation with business.

Women in search of self-esteem, recognition, and approval frequently look toward extramarital affairs as means to achieve such ends. Nearly one half the women interviewed in a study of marital infidelity indicated that the search for self-esteem had been a major factor in their becoming unfaithful.[1] Most approaches to acquiring self-esteem and recognition demand a considerable degree of effort and commitment. Affairs hold some promise of providing instant self-esteem. This is true because approval by significant others is necessary to bolster self-esteem. Positive attitudes toward yourself are a by-product of other peoples having positive attitudes toward you. A woman interprets the advances of a man she respects as concrete evidence that she is a person of worth and attractiveness. As explained by a mother of two adolescent children,

> Until Harry [the man with whom she is having an affair] came
> along I was feeling pretty down on myself. Here I was in the mid-
> dle of a not-so-hot marriage and two almost grown kids. I had
> turned forty and I don't look great in the youth clothing of today.
> I was beginning to think that the only man who would look at me
> was my husband. Then Harry made me feel like I was something
> special. He's young and smart and alive. We only see each other
> about once every two weeks, but it's enough to make me feel like
> a whole person.

There is a seeming paradox inherent in the observation that
affairs elevate self-esteem, as explained by Morton Hunt:

> . . . How can a secret, disloyal, and (according to the Christian
> ethic) immoral act raise one's self-esteem? Yet it does, even while
> creating guilt and self-contempt, for the esteem and the contempt
> apply to different areas of the self—the latter to the woman's moral
> being, the former to her femininity and sexuality.[2]

Normal desires to participate in the new morality or "sexual
revolution" is yet another factor that encourages women to have
extramarital affairs. Women who married as virgins sometimes develop slow-burning resentment about being born too late to
participate in the new morality. Some women under the surface
are jealous of the sexual adventures of their teen-age daughters.
Monogamy makes some women, as well as men, feel culturally de-
prived. Adultery then becomes the solution of choice to participate
in today's sexual morality.

How Many Wives Have Affairs?

Statistical surveys of sexual practice hold considerable appeal because they provide rough guidelines as to what constitutes "normal"
behavior. One general finding from these surveys is that approximately one out of three wives has at least one extramarital affair
during the life span of her marriage. Curiously, the same percentage
of homemakers are discontent with their role in life. We do not
know for sure if it is the same women who are both discontent
and unfaithful. Data supporting the conclusion that about one
third of married women have extramarital affairs comes from several independent sources.

Psychology Today conducted an exhaustive study about sexual

attitudes and practice in 1970. People completing their questionnaires tended to be well educated, politically liberal, young, and
of relatively high income. Sixty-four percent of the women re-
sponding claimed they had not participated in extramarital intercourse, while 36 percent said they had. In terms of the number of
men involved the breakdown is as follows: 13 percent had extramarital intercourse with one male, 11 percent with two or three
males, 5 percent with four to five males, and 7 percent with six or
more males.[3] Most studies suggest that males show a higher inci-
dence of adultery than females. Men and women in *Psychology
Today's* study were about equally unfaithful. Several years ago
the Institute for Sex Research at Indiana University concluded that
35 to 40 percent of wives engage in extramarital affairs.[4] Albert
Ellis, a prominent sexologist, suggests that about one in five married
women commits adultery.[5] His findings are based upon his observations as a practitioner rather than upon the self-reports of women
filling out questionnaires.

Bare statistical information about sexual practices provides limited
insight and understanding about which women are prone to commit adultery. More helpful is an examination of factors, situations,
or life circumstances that predispose or facilitate women toward
marital infidelity. For example, it is both more understandable and
socially acceptable for a woman married twelve years rather than
six months to have an affair even though both women might be
frustrated by homemaking. An implicit assumption here is that
although one out of three married women commits adultery, such
behavior is infrequent and therefore less acceptable among the
newly married. Next we will examine several factors and circumstances that predispose women toward infidelity.

Age, as reflected in years of marriage, is related to adultery.
Women in their thirties and forties show a higher inclination toward
adultery than do women much younger or older than themselves.
Newlyweds might have more guilt about extramarital affairs; on the
positive side they are usually more romantically involved with their
spouses. Older women are more accepting of the status quo and
sometimes have fewer opportunities for affairs.

Social class status has a curious relationship to extramarital affairs
for both men and women. Middle class people have more moral

inhibitions against adultery than do lower and upper class people. Poor and rich people lead more diverse sex lives than do middle class people. This is true despite the much-publicized suburban mate-swapping parties, and the "moral decay" of the middle class suburbs. Closely related to social class is education. Women of high educational level (college graduates and above) and women of low educational level (high school dropouts) are more prone to commit adultery than women of average education (high school graduate).

Personal values and attitudes might be the most important single factor guiding women in their decision to have or not have extra-marital affairs. More traditional, conservative, and puritanical women less frequently practice adultery than do more liberal-minded women. The same women who are tolerant of new life styles (e.g. who accept the idea that some people would prefer to be hippies than suburban housewives) are also more permissive in their sexual orientation. Religious beliefs also can have an impact upon married women's predisposition toward adultery. Fundamentalists, to cite the extreme case, might be concerned about their afterlife if they violated the Seventh Commandment. Unitarians, who lack a systematized set of religious beliefs and rules of conduct underlying their life, might experience less fear about the consequences of adultery.

Adequacy of the marital relationship has a potent effect upon a woman's predisposition to commit adultery. Women whose husbands frustrate their emotional needs frequently seek out opportunities for relationships with other males. Similarly, breakdowns in husband-wife communication predispose both partners toward infidelity. As explained earlier, adultery is more often a symptom than a cause of marital difficulty.

Finally, availability of male companionship has some relationship to frequency of marital infidelity. The fur trapper's wife may be discontent, bored, liberal in her thinking, and dislike her husband, yet the opportunity for unfaithfulness does not present itself. Suburban housewives might commit adultery in higher proportion if more males were available in the suburbs during the day (and if suburban daytime affairs could be conducted more discreetly). Urban dwellers and women whose daily life takes them into contact with men are at an advantage (or disadvantage, depending upon your personal values) in terms of the opportunity for male companionship. Opportunity is a powerful motivator to action, particularly in the sexual sphere. The sentiments expressed in the following comment may be representative of many women:

> How do I feel about affairs? Not too strong either way, but what my husband doesn't know won't hurt him. I'm normal, I won't let a good opportunity go by. Once my husband took the children with him on a fishing trip. One of his business friends came to town and called for him. I guess we were both lonely, but whatever the reason I had my first affair. I don't feel guilty and I wouldn't give up my home for anything.

Combining the psychological and sociological reasons why women have extramarital affairs, the woman most prone to commit adultery would fit the following description. *She is thirty-four years old, wealthy, a graduate from a progressive liberal arts college, liberal in her attitudes toward a variety of social issues, has a career that places her in frequent contact with men, has difficulties in communicating with her husband, and feels frustrated, lonely and bored.*

Have an Affair with Your Husband

Women driven to have extramarital affairs because of discontents stemming from their marital relationship, both sexual and nonsexual, have one option at home worth exploring. In the words of authoress Lois Bird, "Become a happily married mistress."[6] According to this strategy, the affair is one solution to boredom and restlessness but your husband becomes your lover. You become his mistress. Revitalizing your marriage (and yourself in the process) by behaving in a sexually alluring manner toward your husband is an ancient concept. Two thousand years ago in India the doctrine of *Kama Sutra* was taught to newlyweds for the purpose of enhancing the probability of marital success. *Kama Sutra* focuses on sexual and other sensuous pleasures. Indian (Asiatic) maidens were apprised of sixty-four steps they must perform to provide absolute satisfaction to their husbands. Modern day encyclopedias of sex could have been written based upon the information contained in this ancient doctrine. Many of the sexual positions illustrated via statuary and wall carvings suggest *Kama Sutra* was prepared by male chauvinists of their time.

Feminists and feminist sympathizers, both male and female, would regard as atavistic the notion that women should dramatize their femininity in order to please their husbands. According to current thought and sentiment, the modern woman is not a sexual possession of her husband. Exaggerating her femininity in order to satisfy male ego and sexual needs is to become traditional, old-fashioned, and even worse, prostituted. Arousing your husband's physical desires by wearing bikini underwear and perfume is perceived as anathema to the cause of psychological equality, and to some extent as phoniness. There is some validity to the argument that behaving like a mistress toward your husband is old-fashioned, unauthentic, and male-chauvinistic in underlying philosophy. Pendulums of social change, however, swing in both directions. Part of the backlash against the new femininity might be for women to dramatize their femininity in relationships with their husbands. Each woman must decide whether such strategy will benefit her unique situation. Following are several situations in which the woman behaves according to the tenets of "becoming a happily married mistress." Each situation is accompanied by the chief arguments for and against such behavior on the wife's part.

Greeting Husband

Although harassed by a difficult day of her own, the woman makes specific preparation for the husband who has been away for several days. Upon his arrival she is smartly dressed, carefully groomed, and the house appears neat and arranged. She comments, "It's really fine to have you home. I've prepared supper for the children. After they have gone to bed you and I can dine together. Why don't you relax now; let me mix you a drink. Tell me about your trip."

In defense of this strategy, the husband will feel relaxed, flattered, important, and masculine. Rare is the male who would not feel positive about this special treatment. Equally important, he will exhibit reciprocal behavior. Affection and attention directed toward another normal adult (including a spouse) elicits affection and attention in return. The husband will probably reciprocate by doing something special for his wife and show particular interest in her problems. In short, the women psychologically "get her turn;" she is provided the opportunity to discuss her problems and concerns. Additionally, for many people being warm and affectionate toward another individual is a reward in itself.

In opposition to this strategy is the argument that such behavior smacks of phoniness and suppression of real feelings. The emotionally sophisticated woman should make no special effort to appear glamorous upon the husband's return unless she *really feels* like appearing glamorous. If under stress herself she should greet the returning husband with this open and honest statement:

> You have probably had a difficult trip. Well so have I. This week has been ghastly, and I'm almost climbing the walls. I've arranged for a baby sitter. If you feel like going out with me, great. If not, I'll go to a movie or visit a friend. Why don't you make me a drink, I'm awfully busy.

Having accomplished this honest expression of feelings the woman can enjoy the husband's presence. If suppressed, these feelings will create tension in the woman, thus interfering with a relaxed relationship with her husband.

Sexual Intercourse

Whatever verbal or nonverbal communication our next couple transmits, it is apparent to both that tonight they will have sexual relations. Early in the evening husband and wife share in coping with a household emergency; the basement has flooded and one hour of physical labor is required for cleaning up the aftermath. After this dreary task has been accomplished the wife takes a bath, dons a negligee, puts on makeup and a wig, wears perfume, and turns on the record player. She calls out to her husband, "Are you ready?" and an evening of romance begins. During sexual relations she verbally expresses enjoyment to the husband, even at one point *pretending* to have reached an orgasm.

Defending this woman's sexual strategy would have been easier in the 1950's and 60's than in the 70's; nevertheless there is much to recommend it from the male viewpoint. Visual images sexually stimulate males. Women who optimize their physical attractiveness capitalize upon this basic fact of human behavior. Female cleanliness is almost an aphrodisiac for most males, despite the protests of naturalists. Bathing thus enhances marital relationships, whether done alone by the woman or in companionship with the husband. The woman expressing verbal appreciation also has some merit from a motivational standpoint. Much of male sexual capacity, within limits, is psychological in origin. Compliments tend to reinforce good performance and enhance male self-confidence. Women who say to their mate during intercourse, "Honey that was good," are almost guaranteed of repeat performances then or at a later date.

Vehement opposition can also be stated toward this woman's tactics. First, it was unnatural of her to take a bath before sex unless she wanted to take a bath for general reasons. Nature does not require women to bath before mating. Did you ever see a dog, cat, chipmunk, or chimpanzee take a bath before mating? Additionally, there is something earthy and wholesome about an unbathed woman. Only a male imbued with the philosophy that women are sexual objects and household mistresses thinks female cleanliness is an aphrodisiac. Authentic, nonphony, honest women do not have special wardrobes for sex. Negligees, wigs, and perfume make a burlesque out of sexual intercourse. Furthermore, no woman should be required to behave as a prostitute in her own home.

Faking orgasm and other forms of false verbal praise, it can be argued, contribute to dishonest relationships between man and woman. The deception in such a relationship can only be destructive in the long range. Women who fail to reach a climax should unhesitatingly tell this to their spouse in order that he can learn to correct his mistakes. This is a basic principle of learning theory; we correct mistakes by receiving feedback on our performance. "Mood music" also has no place in the bedroom unless both partners enjoy music for its own sake. Closeness of the two people is all the stimulation that is required. Music as an accompaniment to sex contributes about as much to the quality of the relationship as does a water bed or pornographic movies. All are unnecessary where there is mutual love and respect. Sexual relations should not be artificial.

Doing Special Favors for Your Husband

Woman X recognizes that her psychological and physical relationship with her husband leaves much to be desired. Following the philosophy behind "Have an affair with your husband," she asks herself, "What am I doing wrong that could possibly have damaged our relationship?" She decides that by improving her performance as a helpmate, she will be more cherished by her husband. Cherished women, she feels, are treated with more affection and understanding; consequently they are the recipients of better emotional and physical relationships. Her campaign to improve as a helpmate includes arranging for her husband's medical and dental appointments, taking the initiative to entertain his business acquaintances, and clipping newspaper articles relevant to his job. Completing her strategy, she even makes it a practice to invite her mother-in-law to lunch once a month.

Providing the husband does not resent or rebel at becoming too dependent upon his wife there is much to recommend this strategy. Normal males will reciprocate such special favors and there will be more areas in which the couple can express genuine appreciation toward each other. Mutual appreciation strengthens relationships.

Counter-arguments can be offered to the strategy of performing special favors for your husband in order to improve the marital relationship. Feminists argue, and research evidence supports them, that relationships of equalization are necessary to form sound marital adjustment. By performing more and more tasks and errands for the husband, the woman places herself in a subservient role. Many marital difficulties have their genesis in the woman's dearth of interests of her own. The ultimate solution in this situation is for the woman to develop independent interests. Deepening her position as an appendage of her husband can only damage the relationship further.

Affairs Are Constructive and Destructive

Adultery, similar to most complex human relationships, is neither all beneficial nor all harmful. Extramarital affairs have both constructive and destructive elements. Affairs are constructive in the sense that they provide some relief to the problems that motivate women to have affairs. Based upon our earlier analysis of why housewives turn to adultery, it follows that affairs provide these benefits:

1. Boredom, monotony, and loneliness might have some respite,

even if these feelings have their origin in nonsexual areas. Sex, at a minimum, is a good diversion from the drudgery of daily routine.

2. Emotional needs not being met in a strained marital relationship are met by the lover or sweetheart. Affection, understanding, and compassion are often forthcoming from an affair.

3. Expression of revenge and hostility directed toward the husband via the affair could provide some temporary emotional satisfaction. Instead of feelings of anger and revenge remaining suppressed, they are indirectly expressed by transferring affection to another man.

4. Desires for self-esteem, recognition, and approval receive some gratification. Affairs, particularly in their early stages, are characterized by both parties' feeling important and wanted. As they grow older, affairs sometimes fall prey to the hazards of many long-term relationships between man and woman—apathy, indifference, and boredom.

5. Having an affair gives some women the feeling that they are finally participating in society's new sexual largesse. Similarly, many middle class people are beginning to feel "square" and traditional if they have never used marijuana. Homemakers, similar to the youth culture, want an equitable share (or at least a sampling) of what is widely practiced in contemporary society.

6. Finally, to have an affair for many women is simply *fun*. Providing the partner is a man the woman cares for, sexual relations at its most elemental level falls into the category of enjoyment, amusement, recreation, and playful activity. As expressed by the woman to her lover after their first sexual adventure together, "Thank you, that was fun."

Extramarital affairs are not without disadvantage or destructive consequence. Potential disadvantages (the term "potential" implies that some women will be so affected, but not all) of adultery for women follow:

1. Guilt feelings plague many women who engage in extramarital sex. These guilt feelings originate from early cultural and religious conditioning. Committing adultery violates the teaching of your parents and the church. Women vary dramatically in the strength of their conscience; thus guilt is not a universal problem. Feelings of having betrayed your spouse are closely related to guilt feelings

and in many cases are psychologically equivalent mechanisms.

2. Disclosure of the affair to the husband, either intentionally or unintentionally, can lead to major disruptions in the family life style that are both unwanted and unintended by the woman. Separation and/or divorce are often precipitated by disclosure of adultery. Even if separation or divorce are not forthcoming, deterioration of the marital relationship ensues unless the husband is unusually compassionate and understanding.

3. Harmful physical consequences cannot be dismissed from consideration. Women who become pregnant as a consequence of an affair are confronted with a host of difficult decisions. Case histories have been recorded of attempted suicides by women in this entanglement. More flexible abortion laws have already served to decrease the proportion of women who experience neurotic depression because of pregnancy; thus suicide becomes a more remote possibility. Venereal disease is another potential negative consequence of marital infidelity. Modern drugs diminish the harmful effects of this disease but contracting venereal disease could compound the problems of guilt feelings. Physical violence directed toward the wife by the husband who learns of his wife's affair is yet another remote possibility.

4. Perhaps the most striking yet subtle negative consequence of the extramarital affair is that it falls short of bringing total life satisfaction to women. Whatever benefits are forthcoming from the affair, it fails dismally as a total solution to the problem of achieving self-fulfillment.

Self-Fulfillment Is Bigger Than Sex

Affairs are not to be dismissed in terms of their specific positive effect of satisfying your needs for novelty, excitement, affection, and relief of boredom. Women attempting the transition this book deals with have more complex needs than these to gratify. Affairs fall short of providing discontented women what is really missing in their lives—a feeling of accomplishment that comes from achieving goals that are meaningful to you and other people.

Men and women whose entire life revolves around the quest for affection, love, and sex have failed to achieve full maturity. Their development has been arrested at less than the highest level. One might ask in rebuttal, What about hippies and folk song writers whose lives revolve around interpersonal relationships and thoughts about sex? Aren't they fulfilled people? Hippie leaders, just like leaders and organizers in any endeavors, invest considerable emotional energy in some cause they think is worthwhile. Love and friendship are important to them, but devotion to their cause also contributes to their sense of self-fulfillment. Hippie followers who are not committed to any particular cause or work are probably not fulfilled people. Similarly folk singers devote much of their thinking to love and sex, but it takes place in the context of higher-level accomplishment—the writing of folk songs.

Erich Fromm has cautioned against the reliance upon love and affection to compensate for lack of achievement in other pursuits:

> Often psychoanalysts see patients whose ability to love and so be close to others is damaged and yet who function very well sexually and indeed make sexual satisfaction a substitute for love because their sexual potency is their only power in which they have confidence. Their inability to be productive in all other spheres of life and the resulting unhappiness is counterbalanced and veiled by their sexual activities.[7]

Despite this provocative statement by an eminent psychoanalytic thinker, and the widespread belief that women must find broader satisfactions in life than homemaking, the implications of one subtle statement made earlier must be carefully examined. *Self-fulfillment stems from a feeling of accomplishment that comes from achieving goals that are meaningful to you and other people.* Our research strongly suggests that for many women homemaking is meaningful and that many men value the contribution made by full-time homemakers to society. Perhaps two thirds of all homemakers are contented with their role in life. This phenomenon important enough to warrant separate attention.

NOTES

1. Morton Hunt, "Unfaithful Wives: the Reasons Why," *Family Circle*, Apr. 1970, pp. 17-20.
2. *Ibid.*, p. 19.
3. Robert Athanasiou, Phillip Shaver, and Carol Tarvis, "Sex," *Psychology Today*, July 1970, pp. 39-52.
4. Morton Hunt, *op. cit.*, p. 17.
5. Albert Ellis, "Why One Out of Five Wives Is Having an Affair," *Pageant*, Sept. 1967, pp. 114-117.

6. Lois Bird, *How to Be a Happily Married Mistress*, New York, Doubleday, 1971.
7. Erich Fromm, "Sex and Character: the Kinsey Report Viewed from the Standpoint of Psychoanalysis," *Sexual Behavior in American Society*, p. 307, quoted in Betty Friedan, *The Feminine Mystique*, Dell, 1970, p. 267.

Chapter 8

CONTENTED HOMEMAKERS

It is a good horse that never stumbles,
And a good wife that never grumbles.

JOHN RAY
English Proverbs (1670)

What Rewards Stem from Homemaking?

F ULL-TIME homemaking is a fulfilling and rewarding life for many women. Contented homemakers choose not to hear the pleas of the feminists about the plight of women at home. Approximately one quarter to one third of full-time homemakers fall into the "contented" category. They stand in vivid contrast to the one quarter to one third of women who suffer the housewife syndrome. Most women fall somewhere in the middle with respect to their attitudes about homemaking. Each woman who finds fulfillment in the homemaker role has her own unique combination of reasons for this feeling. Seven key reasons some women find contentment in the homemaking role will be explored next. These reasons help one understand the phenomenon of the contented homemaker.

Child rearing is unequivocally the major source of satisfaction in the homemaker role for most women. Providing for children is also an important motivating force behind many women *remaining* in the homemaker function. Taking care of children is thus the *raison d'etre* behind homemaking. Lending credence to this observation are the acute adjustment problems faced by many women when their children are no longer dependent upon them. The arrival of grandchildren again legitimatizes the homemaker role, but the interim period is one in which homemaking seems to lack major purpose.

132

Child rearing is inherently rewarding; and some aspects of child rearing are more rewarding than others. Guiding, teaching, and stimulating the creativity of children provide the deepest rewards, while disciplining or arguing with children provides limited rewards. Psychologically sophisticated mothers have derived considerable personal reward from putting principles of child development into practice (and observing them work). Mother B in the following interchange successfully applies principles recommended by Haim Ginott in *Between Parent and Child* and will thus receive intellectual and emotional rewards. Intellectual rewards, in this situation, stem from correctly applying a child psychology technique. Emotional rewards stem from helping a child with his feelings. Mother A will simply experience frustration.

Steve, a ten-year-old boy, comes to the dinner table with a frown and grumbles that he is not hungry.

> *Mother A:* Steve, are you pouting again? Go stay down in the basement until you can act like a human being. I can't stand boys in an ugly mood.
> *Steve:* Good, I don't want to eat dinner with you anyway.
> *Mother A:* Get out of here right away.
> *Mother B:* Steve, you look angry. Tell me what you are angry about.
> *Steve:* I am angry. Tommy said I throw a baseball like a little girl. He's stupid and I don't like him.
> *Mother B:* That must be very upsetting to you. Perhaps you and Dad can work on your throwing after dinner. Even if you are upset I would like you to eat dinner now with the rest of the family.

Satisfying mother-child activities, in general, are those in which both mother and child participate in a joint activity to reach a common goal. For example, both a mother and her five-year-old daughter will find more reward in solving a jigsaw puzzle together than if the mother makes a dress for the daughter. Shared activities are more rewarding than unilateral activities in child rearing as well as in other phases of life.

Homemakers who take pride in raising children are not without encouragement from prestigious figures. As stated by Dr. Joyce Brothers,

> . . . Have respect for your job. In our largely male-oriented culture, motherhood is sometimes made to seem less important—at any

rate, less impressive—than running a corporation or practicing law. But no job is more demanding, more creative, more ultimately worthwhile than producing a healthy, happy child. The hand that rocks the cradle really does rule the world.[1]

Satisfaction of desires for security, love, and affection is an important reward derived from marriage for many women. Security needs are satisfied because marriage and motherhood promise more stable relationships with people than do less formal living arrangements. This is still true despite the steadily increasing proportion of marriages that terminate in divorce or separation. Desires for financial as well as emotional security often represent reasons for women seeking out marriage. Thus even imperfect marital relationships offer the reward of satisfying a financial motive.

Husband and children provide women an appropriate outlet for behaving affectionately toward others and receiving affection in return. Mother-child relationships hold particularly true in this regard. However inept a woman might be in her interpersonal relationships, it remains a universally accepted truth that she is loved by her children and that she loves her children. Marriage thus provides a captive audience for expressing and receiving love and affection. Contented homemakers consider this to be an important reward.

One thirty-two-year-old woman, reflecting upon the positive aspects of her life, made the following comments:

> The most rewarding thing that I find as a housewife is having a pal—a friend—a real true friend. It's the walks in the park, or the nights at home when I can tell him all my problems and he tells me his. It's—and I hate to use this cliche—being able to bare one's soul to another without fear that he will laugh or criticize.[2]

Independence and freedom of action is yet another important reward found in the homemaker's role. Despite the many demands placed upon a homemaker, she still has substantial blocks of time to manage as she sees fit. "Your time's your own" and "You can set your own schedule and your own pace" are themes frequently appearing in the reactions of contented homemakers to their roles. Implied here is not that homemaking places light demands upon the woman. Contented homemakers feel there are many demands placed upon them, but that they determine the sequence in which activities will be performed. Women who have worked outside the home in jobs where others set the work pace for them are particularly appreciative of the autonomy offered by homemaking.

Contributing to this feeling of autonomy is the absence of working under the close scrutiny of a supervisor. Notice the needs for autonomy in this statement: "What do I really like about being a housewife? It's great not to have somebody breathing down your neck all day. Nobody watches every move I make. Maybe in some ways my husband is the boss, but at least he's not around all day."

The feelings of autonomy and freedom found in running a home would be difficult to duplicate except in situations where a woman might become the proprietor of a small store. Executives in almost every organization have their decisions reviewed and their results measured by other people. One might argue that, unlike the company executive's situation, nobody *cares* what the homemaker does. Contented homemakers, however, have a much more positive attitude toward their role in life.

Mastery over one's environment is a normal need found in most people. Homemaking in some small way provides many women an outlet for this need. Many tasks performed within the context of homemaking provide women the feeling of having accomplished something that required an above average degree of skill. Chapter 5, "Improving the Homemaking Task," discussed desirable versus undesirable homemaking tasks. In general, those activities which provide some opportunity for the expression of creativity and individuality are sources of ego satisfaction. Despite the plethora of antihomemaking sentiment expressed today, many women derive personal satisfaction from activities such as hostessing parties and interior decorating. Contented homemakers look at their role with enough objectivity to accept the idea that some portions of their work are inherently satisfying.

Many contented housewives find satisfaction in having mastered skills previously unfamiliar to them. Except when a woman has homemaking responsibilities thrust upon her as an adolescent, new skills have to be developed during marriage. Several women in our survey lamented that their job required as much "job knowledge" as many positions with higher status and pay.

The feminine mystique is alive and real for many women. Millions of women still cling to the culturally imbedded notion that their fulfillment in life can best be derived from the full-time pursuit of homemaking. Motherhood, wifehood, and housekeeping to them constitute the "American Dream." Becoming a wife, mother, and "lady of the house" is the only vehicle by which the feminine mystique can be realized. Thus homemaking contributes to contentment and inner tranquility for large numbers of women in our society. Contented homemakers are not ashamed to admit that maintaining a home and raising a family form an important life goal for them.

The proportion of college women who idealize marriage and child rearing is undoubtedly diminishing. Philip E. Slater, a prominent sociologist, has observed that his women students see little appeal in marriage as it presently exists.[3] Large numbers of college women have male roommates and make no attempt to legitimatize their relationship by assuming it will evolve into marriage. Yet there are still large numbers of college women remaining who are actively in search of a husband and to whom the feminine mystique represents a desirable life pattern. One twenty-year-old co-ed made this illuminating comment:

> Yes, I'm all for women's liberation. I'm a member of the local group. But don't think all my friends believe the way I do. If you talked to these girls and if they were honest with you, you'd see what I mean. Many of these girls are here to find a husband. It's the same thing it's always been.

Assuming that these girls find a compatible husband, raise children, and tend to housekeeping chores, they will join the ranks of contented homemakers Similarly the eighteen-year-old man who establishes dentistry as his major life goal experiences a degree of contentment and satisfaction when eight years later he becomes a full-fledged dentist. He may develop other goals, such as officership in a local dental association, but psychologically he has arrived.

Homemaking provides ample opportunities to gratify service needs. Desires to serve, nurture, take care of, or please other people are embedded in the psychological makeup of many women (and men). This need to serve has many appropriate outlets in society. Social work, nursing, elementary school teaching, special education, and a variety of hospital volunteer positions give one an ample opportunity to provide for the welfare of others. Homemaking, however, is the role with the most continuous opportunities for gratifying such needs. Assisting a husband in his career is yet another outlet for a woman's desire to help others.

Homemaking has been criticized as a life situation in which the mother is forced to spend much of her time tending to the physical needs of husband and children. Yet taking away some homemakers' opportunity to provide for the needs of others would be as damaging to them as would be taking away career opportunities from feminists.

Most readers are probably familiar with the woman who stifles the growth toward independence of her children (and sometimes husband) because of her needs to nurture them. Some infants are inhibited in their walking because their mothers insist on carrying them. Other women delight in tending to concerns such as the diet and dress of their husbands. Husbands, of course, may benefit from such ministrations by their wives, but the wives' needs are being taken care of simultaneously. Note the service motivation underlying this woman's analysis of the rewards she receives from homemaking:

> My rewards are making my husband happy and healthy and helping my children grow up. The rewards of a housewife are hard to talk about. They're not material. They're something inside a woman that a man could never know or understand. It's just a feeling that I am doing what I'm supposed to be doing and helping others at the same time.[4]

Rewards stemming from homemaking are less glamorous than those attainable in occupations such as gynecology, psychiatry, television announcing, writing, or politics. Unfortunately most homemakers would not occupy such glamorous roles if they either left homemaking or had never entered homemaking. Critics of modern feminists have noted that the strongest objections to full-time homemaking are raised by women with the talent and education required to participate in more glamorous and rewarding occupations. Most women in the contented homemaker category would not find careers with abundant opportunity for self-expression if they did enter the outside world. Many women, for example, find elementary school teaching to be more frustrating than rewarding. To those frustrated by teaching, homemaking is a pleasant alternative. There are former secretaries, file clerks, insurance underwriters, key punch operators, and sometimes even airline stewardesses who find more rewards in homemaking than they found in their jobs.

Contented homemakers also recognize that every action they take in their homes in some way directly benefits either themselves or other family members. Working in somebody else's organization does not provide the same opportunity. One woman from Maine, familiar with both homemaking and career roles, offers the following advice to homemakers:

> If you ever, ever begin to suspect that housewifery is nothing but unglamorous drudgery—think of the glamorous secretary tripping down the street in her expensive suits and her expensive shoes with her hair all wound up in lustrous coils—slaving daily for some guy she isn't even married to! In an office that is never hers! For people she is not related to! And helping to earn money that will never remotely settle in her bank account At least, dear woman, what you work upon is yours, the meals you plan you get the credit for, the house you shine reflects your personality, the children are your children, and the man—your man![5] *

This woman has presented an idealized version of the pride of ownership that is feasible in carrying out homemaking chores. Beneath her exaggerated statement is the fundamental truth that many women prefer to be their own boss. Rewards stemming from this aspect of the homemaker role are not dissimilar to those a candy store owner receives in running his business. Hours are long, pay is modest, but at least he feels some pride of ownership.

What Kind of a Person Is the Contented Homemaker?

Women of many different types are contented homemakers. Included in their ranks are women of different ethnic backgrounds, education, geographic locations, and income. Despite these differences, contented homemakers have enough in common to warrant making a few generalizations about them.

Contented homemakers live in many different parts of the country but they are most frequently found in suburban, middle class housing areas. Suburbs exert a gravitational pull on people who choose the living pattern whereby the husband works outside the home while the wife plays the full-time homemaker role. Rural areas, according to

*Reprinted by permission from *Changing Times*, the Kiplinger Magazine, (April, 1965 issue). Copyright 1965 by The Kiplinger Washington Editors, Inc., 1729 H Street, N.W., Washington, D.C. 20006.

some tentative evidence we have collected, show a high proportion of contented homemakers. Many rural women have only a vague intellectual appreciation of what other options in life are open for them. Full-time homemaking thus is the only logical life style to which they aspire. To be discontent—except when it stems from some type of physical pain—requires some standard of comparison. Farm women are thus more content with the homemaking role.

Educationally, contented homemakers are usually high school graduates with perhaps one to two years of college. Women with more extensive formal education often experience discontentment because their education is under-utilized. Reasons underlying why a woman attended college to some extent shape her later attitudes about whether or not this education is wasted. Girls whose motives for attending college were mostly social are less concerned about using their education than girls whose motives were intellectual.

Sex is closely related to contentment with the homemaker role. Almost no males in our culture admit to being satisfied with full-time homemaking for themselves. Role reversals whereby the wife works outside the home and her husband tends the home and children occur primarily in times of recession. Coal miners, physicists, and engineers all have been known to suffer bruised egos and injured self-images when forced into full-time homemaking by economic circumstance.

Family income has a curious relationship to contentment with full-time homemaking. Women managing households where finances are a major problem have many discontentments because of money problems. Women in wealthier families devote less time to homemaking and are therefore more content with their total life style. Stripped of their diverse activities, they might show more discontentment with homemaking. Contented homemakers are found in highest proportion among the middle income ranks. The wife of a junior executive takes pride in managing family finances and making wise purchase for the family. Any major expenditures at this income level warrant careful financial planning by both husband and wife. Luxuries such as unexpected gifts or dining in expensive restaurants are rare enough to represent sources of satisfaction to women at moderate income levels. Wealthier women develop more cavalier attitudes toward minor luxuries. Dissatisfaction would quickly ensue, however, should these luxuries be taken away.

Personal traits, values, and attitudes reveal more about the contented homemaker than do the demographic characterists just described. Intelligence, as reflected in extent of formal education, is generally above average but not typically superior among these contented women. Most of their personality characteristics fall into the "average" category. Contented homemakers, for example, tend to show medium amounts of assertiveness and aggressiveness. They are sufficiently assertive to seek solutions to their problem, but their assertiveness and aggressiveness do not compel them into frequent disputes with other people. These women do not feel strongly competitive toward their husbands and children for recognition; thus another source of potential frustration in their lives is eliminated.

Traditional, middle class values about a variety of topics characterize contented homemakers. Rarely are they vehemently anti any thing or institution unless that thing or institution threatens their middle class way of life. Thus contented homemakers do not champion the cause of political activists on either the left or right. They either oppose or barely tolerate women's liberation. Drugs and drug-like substances, other than alcohol, tobacco, and medicines, are looked upon with disfavor and sometimes disbelief by them.

Contented homemakers are generally average in femininity and needs for accomplishment. Vivid contrasts can be drawn between the contented homemaker and the women's liberationist described in Chapter 2. The former stand at the other end of the continuum from the latter on most major personality characteristics and personal attitudes. Basically, feminists are discontent with women's role in society, while contented homemakers like it just fine. Feminists, to provide one more illustration, are strongly independent, while contented homemakers are more dependent upon other people.

Women classified as contented homemakers, by definition, do not experience the housewife syndrome. Emotional disturbance or illness are also less prevalent among contented homemakers. There are few pressures in their lives, either self-generated or environmental, pushing them toward emotional upset. Considering the good mental health and the freedom from pressures experienced by contented homemakers, it is worth exploring the feasibility of becoming a contented homemaker.

How Do You Become a Contented Homemaker?

More appropriately, it might be asked, should you become a contented homemaker? Your husband and children might prefer that you become a contented homemaker, but whether homemaking as a full-time occupation fits your self-image is your decision. By this point in the book you should have increased your self-knowledge enough to appreciate the extent to which you want to play a multiple role in life. Women described in this chapter find full-time homemaking to be a rewarding and fulfilling experience. Many normal, healthy women will always be discontent with full-time homemaking. The intellectually honest answer to these women is not to attempt to adjust to full-time homemaking.

Adjustment in one sense means making a series of small compromises which in fact avoid the major issue. Men and women with marital difficulties often enter marriage counseling with the expectation that they will emerge better adjusted to each other. Thus both make a series of small compromises and concessions that move the marriage from a position of open warfare back to one of neutrality. Wife A, for example, agrees to be more forthright in discussing points or irritation in the marriage rather than sulking about them. Husband A in turn agrees to tone down his verbal abusiveness when something in the marital relationship disturbs him. These "trade-offs" work well providing they share an underlying mutual respect and admiration. Lacking this core ingredient—mutual caring for each other—adjustment to the marriage represents a continual strain for both partners. Similarly, if you have underlying negative attitudes toward full-time homemaking, find additional outlet for your energies. Serious interests, jobs outside the home, educational experiences, volunteer activities, and in some instances extramarital affairs may represent your unique solution.

Don't put a psychological lid on yourself. Suppression of your discontent will not make you a contented homemaker. More probably you will experience the housewife syndrome. Women discontented with homemaking who attempt to suppress their feelings ultimately become the stereotyped "frustrated housewife."

NOTES

1. Dr. Joyce Brothers, "Is There a Perfect Mother?" *Good Housekeeping*, June 1970, pp. 52-56.

2. I thank David DuBois, a former student of mine, for having gathered this quote.

3. Philip E. Slater, "Must Marriage Cheat Today's Young Women?" *Redbook*, Feb. 1971, pp. 67, 165-167.

4. I thank Thomas A. Posiadlo, a former student of mine, for having gathered this quote.

5. "What Does She Do All Day?" *Changing Times*, Apr., 1965, p. 34.

Chapter 9

DISCONTENT OR DISTURBED?

> *The different sorts of madness are innumerable.*
>
> RABELAIS

This Woman Is Disturbed

WHEN does discontentment with the housewife role indicate emotional disturbance rather than objectively based dissatisfaction with an imperfect role? This is a complex question for which only tentative and approximate answers are available. Our purpose in writing this chapter is to help sensitize you to the difference between normal discontentment and emotional disorder or disturbance. Differentiating between normal versus neurotic reactions requires both professional skill and insight. Clinical psychologists and psychiatrists, in surprisingly high proportion, even question the value of making such differentiation. "Labels" are sometimes thought to interfere with rather than enhance understanding of people. Describing the actual behavior of people sometimes provides more understanding than does placing them into stereotyped categories.

Janet Carson is both discontent *and* disturbed. Her emotional disturbance is reflected in both the intensity and variety of her symptoms.

> Janet was raised by foreign-born parents in a residential section of a medium-sized eastern city. Both she and her brothers were adequately provided for in terms of food, clothing, love, and affection. Both brothers became mechanical engineers, while Janet received a bachelor's degree in fine arts. She worked as an artist in an advertising agency for two years before marrying George Carson, an account executive. Janet became pregnant four months after her marriage date and terminated her employment during her fifth month of pregnancy. Janet and her husband had four children in their

first six years of marriage, two boys and two girls. George remained unavailable for virtually all of the day-by-day care of the children, a situation he attributes to a hectic and demanding work schedule.

Gradually, after the fourth child was born, Janet began to manifest subtle changes in behavior. Her husband noticed that she became less and less concerned about her physical appearance and clothing. She wore the same pair of slacks and blouse almost every day for one month until finally the outfit tore and became unwearable. Her interests in activities outside the home began to diminish. Three attempts by George to take her out to dinner or to visit friends were met with pointed rejection. She withdrew as a regular member of her bridge group and asked a friend to substitute for her in a bowling league. When friends or parents called on the telephone, she abruptly terminated the conversation with a variety of vague excuses. However, Janet one day called her husband at work five times to discuss her concern about losing her artistic talent by being a full-time housewife.

Janet's relationship with her husband and children also manifested profound change. Lack of emotional responsiveness characterized most of her interactions with them. When George inquired about her daily activities or how she was feeling, Janet often retorted, "I really don't feel like talking now." Roger, the oldest child, rushed home one day to share with his mother his excitement about having been selected for the lead in the fifth-grade play. Janet responded, "That doesn't sound interesting to me." Sexual relations with George diminished in intensity and frequency. Even conversing with her husband became an unwanted burden to Janet. Prior to the onset of these changes in behavior, Janet was characterized as talkative and cheerful by her husband and friends. Now she waited for others to take the initiative in conversation, and rarely responded when they talked.

Janet tripled her consumption of alcohol. She began drinking whiskey shortly after lunch and consumed about one pint per day. Her cigarette consumption doubled from one to two packs per day. One day the oldest child said to his father, "I think Mommy is groggy from drinking again."

Janet's description of her feelings underlying these changes in behavior show insight into her situation: "Things were getting pretty bad. I just didn't care anymore. It was such a burden to always worry about how George feels about how I feel. I wanted to reach out and get close to the kids, but I couldn't. Friends became a horrible scene for me. I didn't want to talk to anybody. It was more than I could do to keep the house in shape and take care of myself. I tried to get my work done, but I was just spinning around in circles. I began to wonder if I would ever get back to my art.

"These feelings all seemed to start after the last baby was born. Here I was, stuck to the routine of being trapped in the house with a newborn. I'm too old to start that routine again. I also felt lousy about feeling that way, since it was mostly my idea to have another baby. I began to have these horrible dreams about the baby drowning and I couldn't save her. That really shook me up, like nothing else that has ever happened to me.

"After awhile I didn't even feel tense anymore. Nothing bothered me. I just kind of gave up and felt miserable and alone all the time. When I stopped even caring for myself or the children I finally thought it was time to look for help."

Janet's feelings and behavior suggest that she is neurotically depressed and not simply undergoing a housewife syndrome reaction. No one feeling or action alone is sufficient to characterize her as emotionally disturbed. Nightmares about children drowning, for example, are perhaps more frequent than most parents admit. Simple fear about the child's security could conceivably precipitate dreams about the child drowning; no subconscious homicidal wish is inevitably present in such a dream. Many normal, mentally healthy women at one time or another (for brief periods of time) feel and act like Janet Carson. Mental health, or so-called normal behavior, is difficult to define.

Who Is a Mentally Healthy Woman?

Distinguishing between normal discontents, concerns, and apprehensions on the one hand versus neurotic behavior patterns on the other is a complex skill. Most neurotic people are discontent, but not all discontent people are neurotic. Professional advice should be sought whenever there is serious concern about the mental health status of one person in particular.

Describing what constitutes a mentally healthy woman proceeds best at two levels; first we will approach the problem from the standpoint of an *absence of obvious maladjustment*. Six broad questions one might ask about herself or another person to rule out or rule in behavior disturbance follow.[1] Negative responses to several of these suggest that professional consultation should be sought. Caution must be exercised in interpreting answers to these questions. There is no one-to-one relationship between emotional disorder and negative responses to these questions; they are approximate guidelines. Additionally, any woman might display signs of emotional disorder in her response to a stress situation. Injury or death to a child, for example, may precipitate symptoms of emotional disorder in the strongest person. True neurotic or psychotic reactions are long-standing patterns of behavior. Alcohol and a variety of drugs can also precipitate a temporary, transient state of emotional impairment.

Does the person's behavior seem appropriate to objective circumstances? Learning that you and your husband can no longer retain membership in a golf club because of financial circumstances may be a cause for some concern. Verbal expression of discontentment about this subject directed toward your husband is behavior scaled to the gravity of the situation. However, a week-long tirade about the injustices of the capitalist system suggests behavior inappropriate to the circumstances.

Learning that her mother and father would be visiting her home for a weekend, a woman called in a professional housecleaning service to properly clean her house for this occasion. She also insisted that the entire house be redecorated and that her husband exert influence to find a firm to complete the job within ten days. Once the house was decorated and cleaned, she thought her husband and children should stay in a hotel until her parents arrived. This latter move was designed to insure that the home would be in meticulous order for her parents. Pride in the appearance of the home and a desire to please her parents are normal feelings. Obsessive concern about making preparation for her parents, however, is behavior inappropriate to the circumstances.

Have sudden changes in past behavior patterns taken place? Humans, as well as lower forms of animals, tend to repeat behavior patterns. Considerable effort and self-discipline is required to convert any one personality trait or characteristic to its opposite. Assume Woman A has been a lifelong pet fancier. Sudden derogatory comments by her about pets and physical abuse of them signifies a profound change in behavior. Affection has turned to hostility. Woman B has been a serious student of contemporary fiction throughout her adult life. She belongs to two book clubs and reviews novels for a local newspaper. Suddenly she purges the house of all novels written within the last fifteen years. She proclaims that contemporary works are "simply trash" and that they do not belong in her house. Reading novels, she adds, diverts time that could be better spent in religious study or conversing with family members. Women B is entitled to these beliefs about contemporary fiction and her thinking is not necessarily bizarre. What is a cause for alarm is the turnabout in her attitudes and behavior.

Is the person emotionally resilient? Life, for most people, is beset with a series of crises. Emotional disorder is suggested when a person cannot bounce back (be emotionally resilient) in the face of a minor crisis, setback, or reversal. Attending the funeral of a ninety-year-old grandmother would bring some temporary grief to most women. Remaining depressed about her grandmother's death would suggest an emotional problem. One thirty-three-year-old woman with four children learned from her gynecologist it would be physically unwise for her to have any more children. She reacted to this medical verdict with a despondency that appeared permanent to her husband. In addition, she suffered a weight loss and withdrew from her friends. Prompting by her husband to forget about her problems served to intensify her depressive reaction. Objective analysis of the situation indicates that (a) this woman already has four children and (b) she has passed her physiological prime for child bearing; therefore her depression is unwarranted. Emotional disturbance, unfortunately, is a subjective and personal matter that rarely conforms to objective and logical rules of behavior.

Has emotional control been lost? Emotional expressiveness and spontaneity, within limits, signify good mental health. Shouting in the elevator of your building that you "can't stand it anymore . . . this is a terrible life" suggests emotional difficulty, not spontaneity. Emotions out of control can relate to positive or negative feelings. Negative feelings out of control are typified by temper tantrums and hostile outbursts directed toward the husband and children. Women who exhibit rage reactions upon every disagreement with their children may be bordering on emotional illness. Less prevalent, but still diagnostically significant, is uncontrollable laughter about minor situations. Laughter beyond the requirements of a situation is suggestive of loss of emotional control, particularly if the pattern cannot be reversed upon request. Thus the person who cannot stop laughing even when others have stopped may be under considerable mental strain. Constant need to shower others with affection (particularly people who will not reciprocate this affection) is another manifestation of loss of emotional control. Positive feelings toward other people are important for mental health, but such feelings out of control are symptomatic of personal difficulties.

Can the person explain his or her behavior? People should be able to explain or justify the motives underlying their behavior with some respect for logic and reason. Asked, "Why do you want a divorce from your husband?" one woman replied, "I have no idea." This kind of response is symptomatic of emotional illness, while the response, "Because he's a bastard," is more normal. People are not expected to be fully aware of the motives behind their every action, but logical reasons to justify most behavior should be apparent. These reasons do not have to appear logical and rational to everybody else. One woman and her husband left a traditional suburban way of life to raise pigs in the west. Urban friends of theirs could not fathom the why of their behavior, yet to this couple pig farming represented an important way of getting close to nature and casting aside what they perceived as the confines of suburban living; thus their behavior was not symptomatic of emotional disorder.

Is the person's behavior destructive to themselves or others? Behavior destructive of other people or their property is yet another revealing symptom of emotional illness. Even in childhood, torturing animals or physical abuse of playmates is cause for questioning the individual's mental health status. Legend has it at a large midwestern university that a wife burned and destroyed her husband's doctoral dissertation before it was submitted for final approval. Countering this destructive behavior on his wife's part, he burned down their apartment. Both exhibited destructive behavior beyond the limits of normal behavior. Child battering as a relief of the pressures created by child rearing is a surprisingly frequent yet pathological and destructive symptom of emotional illness.

Destruction of other people can occur at both the physical and psychological levels. Responses such as "You're an idiot" to every disagreement of opinion with another person is psychologically destructive behavior and symptomatic of deep personal conflicts.

Behavior geared toward self-destruction has its physical and psychological manifestations. Physically self-destructive behavior is exemplified by the alcoholic or perhaps by the woman who violates all sound rules of nutrition while on a crash diet. Accident proneness, at home and on the job, has at various times been considered symptomatic of self-destructive behavior. Simple clumsiness and absent-mindedness, however, account for much of what was formerly considered accident proneness. Psychologically self-destructive behavior is illustrated by the woman beset by the housewife syndrome who convinces her husband that they should have another child. Infant rearing will guarantee that she cannot implement the plan she has formulated to reduce the constraints in her life situation.

Mental health is considerably more complex and subtle than the absence of mental disorder. Good muscular coordination, to use a physical analogy, is more complex than the absence of strained, injured, or diseased muscles. Fine wine, as yet another analogy, involves much more than the absence of impurities such as the taste of vinegar. Good mental health connotes about the same meaning as the terms "emotional maturity" and "normal behavior." Next we will suggest guidelines for describing the psychologically healthy person. These manifestations of psychological health follow closely ideas formulated in a classical textbook of abnormal psychology.[2]

Feelings of Security. Healthy people feel secure in relation to their work, family, and friends. Women who do not feel psychologically safe with their spouses and children have a difficult time achieving robust mental health. People feel safest when those around them treat them with acceptance and tolerance. Being rejected by people significant to you creates feelings of insecurity.

Realistic Self-Evaluation. Chapter 4, "Strengthening Your Self-Image," discussed this topic at length, but its importance merits attention again. Realistic opinions about your strengths and weaknesses help guide you toward activities that can enhance your mental health. For example, the forty-year-old widow with three children should evaluate her chances for remarriage in terms of the realities of her situation. Some potential life companions are available for her if she accepts the reality that she is now attractive to a different set of men than she was fifteen years ago. The ambitious and talented woman who rebels at being somebody's assistant should find a position where she can assume the role of boss. Recognizing her problems in being a follower will contribute to her mental health.

Emotional Spontaneity and Expressiveness. Emotionality is the double-edged sword of mental health. Common sense and insight must guide a person toward striking a balance between being warm and spontaneous toward others, yet not being perceived as flighty, hysterical, giddy, or on the other hand tactless and hostile. In relationship to others, emotional spontaneity refers to forming lasting emotional ties such as friendships and love relationships, the ability to empathize with and share other people's feelings, and the ability to confront others with your true feelings without losing control or hurting them in the process.

Contact with Reality. Mentally healthy people are in contact with reality. (Much to the chagrin of the person whose mental health is being judged, the majority defines the boundaries of reality.) This involves first an absence of excessive fantasy; the mentally healthy woman combines action plus fantasy in her approach to life. Second, contact with reality infers a realistic and broad outlook on the world, with the ability to effectively manage and overcome crisis and reversal. Third is the ability to change if external circumstances cannot be modified. Thus the woman who cannot afford the tuition to attend the college of her choice will undertake a home study program until there is improvement in the family financial situation.

Healthy Bodily Desires and the Ability to Gratify Them. Included here are (a) a healthy and positive attitude toward bodily functions in terms of accepting but not being preoccupied with them—people preoccupied with their bodily functions diminish their enjoyment of life and represent a source of boredom to others; (b) ability to derive pleasure from simple activities, such as eating and sleeping, and to bounce back from fatigue; (c) sexual adequacy—healthy people enjoy both participating in and talking about sex without shame or guilt; and (d) ability to keep any physical activity or bodily function within proper perspective and balance. Thus the two-hundred-fifty-pound woman and the nymphomaniac both overindulge in bodily activities.

Integration and Consistency of Personality. This is a catchall concept meaning (a) a well-rounded approach to interests and pastimes; (b) an ability to concentrate enough on projects to follow them through to completion; (c) reasonable predictability and stability in your behavior—for example, other people have difficulty in relating to you if the same behavior on their part elicits opposite behavior from you at different times—the woman who once says to a friend, "Don't ever discuss sex in my house," and later asks, "What affairs have you heard about lately?" winds up confusing and alienating people; and (d) absence of major, all-encompassing personal conflicts.

Adequate Life Goals. Realistic goal setting was mentioned earlier in terms of its contribution to the self-image and self-fulfillment. Establishing and achieving goals also contributes to mental health when it involves (a) achievable, realistic, and compatible (not contradictory or mutually exclusive) goals—a woman who wants to remain married to a man whose work involves frequent job transfers must sacrifice some of her goals for stability in work of her own; (b) reasonable persistence to achieve goals—worthwhile accomplishment in any field entails much patient plodding; and (c) goals which involve some good to society—there is inherent satisfaction in accomplishing things that directly or indirectly help other people.

Ability to Profit from Experience. Mature and healthy people profit from their experiences, but rare is the person who never makes the same mistake twice. People must benefit from their mistakes to improve skills involving both things and people. Frustration and feelings of defeat are inevitable when the same errors block progress more than once. I recall the situation of a woman who married three alcoholics in succession. Underlying these three mistakes was her need to nurture a dependent and helpless male. Until she could learn to find another outlet for this need, her life with men would continue to be a source of personal anguish. Emotionally mature people profit from their experiences even when the overall situation is unpleasant and uncomfortable. The woman who works for an inept manager at least has the opportunity to learn by example how not to manage people. Recently divorced, one woman was encouraged by her friends to join a club for formerly married people. She found the first meeting embarrassing and uncomfortable but came away from the meeting with the insight that organized approaches to meeting men were inconsistent with her self-image.

Adaptation to Group Values. Protests can be heard at this point that "this sounds like a psychologist telling us that the key to good mental health is to become a conformist." Observation of subtle meanings is required to appreciate the difference between conformity and adaptation to group values. Conformists exercise limited judgment of their own, while adaptation to group values infers integrating your own interests with those of your reference groups. Homeowners with children must be willing to allow neighbors' children to play in their yard if they do not want their own children ostracized from the group. Suburban housewives cannot sunbathe nude on their lawns if they value acceptance from friends of the same sex. The emotionally immature woman will regard such restrictions as "conformity," while the more mature person will accept such constraints on behavior as a normal part of societal living. Correspondingly an emotionally mature woman living in an apartment will avoid cooking meals that offend her neighbors' olfactory sensitivities. Women of lesser emotional maturity might be inclined to defend their rights to cook what they please, when they please.

Emancipation from Group Pressures. Adaptation to group standards when carried to extremes is equally unhealthy. Emotionally mature and mentally healthy people feel secure in expressing their individuality and are not concerned with group acceptance on every issue. Emancipation from the group involves (a) at least some originality, individuality, and the ability to exercise your own preferences; (b) expression of your own opinion about salient issues—for example, opposing the legalization of marijuana when the group favors such action, or vice versa; (c) the absence of excessive need for approval from the group in terms of reassurance and flattery; and (d) an ability to tolerate value systems and beliefs different from those of your group—thus the feminist who does not ridicule the woman who prefers to be a full-time homemaker is emotionally mature.

When Should a Person Enter Psychotherapy?

Assume your tentative self-assessment up to this point suggests that your mental health requires substantial improvement. Although the safety of yourself and others is not in question (if this were true, others would have recommended help by now), your ability to cope with your problems, concerns, and conflicts seems limited. Remaining is the question, When—at what point—do you seek professional help with your problems? This is a highly personal matter, but several important factors should enter into this decision.

First, you must be motivated to want to change. Any form of therapeutic intervention proceeds more swiftly when the client or patient has a genuine desire to change and improve. Reflecting about some of the guidelines for measuring adequate mental health may help you establish the proper motivation. Being forced into psychotherapy is bad for three people—you, the person who forced you, and the therapist.

Second, if you are properly motivated, the sooner you enter therapy the better are your chances for improvement. This is a common sense principle well supported by research. Problems should be dealt with before they become unmanageable. Disturbed behavior patterns of long standing are more difficult to modify than those of recent onset.

Third, the opinion of people you respect and with whom you have a close relationship should carry some weight in making the decisions both about when and *if* to enter therapy. Intimate friends and spouse should be able to give you an informed opinion about recent changes in your behavior or emotional responses. Admittedly, your friends and spouse are emotionally involved with you and are probably not professional diagnosticians. However, observations by people who know you will represent an invaluable source of information in formulating a diagnosis.

Which professional specialist to consult is another decision facing the person seeking psychotherapy. Practitioners from four overlapping disciplines offer psychotherapy to the public, although most private practice of psychotherapy is conducted by psychiatrists and clinical psychologists. *Psychiatrists* are medical specialists who among their mental health services provide drug therapy and psychotherapy. Psychiatry is a branch of medicine and all psychiatrists are medical doctors. According to the American Medical and American Psychiatric Associations, disturbances in behavior are classified as diseases, as are chicken pox and brain tumors. Recent thinking (particularly that generated by psychologists) regards most emotional difficulties as maladaptive behavior that is learned and must therefore be unlearned. Emotional illness is thus no more a disease than are poor work habits.

Psychoanalysts may be either psychiatrists or clinical psychologists who have attended an institute to acquire the additional specialty of psychoanalysis—an extensive, long-term psychotherapy geared toward the actual reconstruction of personality. Orthodox psychoanalytic therapy is gradually becoming extinct. Briefer forms of counseling and therapy that focus more upon the present than the past have begun to replace psychoanalysis. Researchers have for many years taken a dim view of the benefits of psychoanalysis, thus adding to its decreasing popularity. In its defense, psychoanalysis has made a substantial contribution to modern thought about the nature of man. Most theories of personality stem from psychoanalytic doctrine and most forms of psychotherapy owe their heritage to psychoanalysis.

Clinical psychologists are psychologists who specialize in the diagnosis and treatment of emotional disorder. Generally they are Ph.D.'s in psychology, with some research training. There is considerable overlap between the work of clinical psychologists and psychiatrists. Both use methods developed by each other, although many rivalries and jealousies exist between these two professions. Psychologists are licensed in many states to diagnose and treat emotional disorder, but only psychiatrists (and any other medical practitioner) are lawfully permitted to dispense drugs. Psychology, as a branch of science, provides the knowledge base for psychiatry and clinical psychology.

Psychiatric social workers conduct most of the actual psychotherapy that takes place in many mental health settings, but they are infrequently found in private practice. Similar to psychiatrists, much of the knowledge base in their field stems from abnormal and social psychology. Typically these practitioners have a master's degree, but some have Ph.D.'s in social work. In institutional settings social workers combine forces with psychiatrists and psychologists to provide full service to the patient.

Research evidence pointedly indicates that the competence and experience of the therapist and the quality of your relationship with him (or her) are the crucial determinants of the outcome of psychotherapy. Where he received his degree or the nature of his particular academic specialty is of less significance. Whether or not psychotherapy will be successful for you depends to a large extent upon you, the skill of the therapist, and the suitability of his approaches for you.

Approaches to psychotherapy are many and varied. Some emphasize lengthy discussions of the past, while others focus on current conflicts and concerns. Psychotherapy takes place in both group and individual sessions. Behavior therapies focus on the client or patient's overcoming maladaptive behavior patterns such as a stutter or specific fear. Therapists differ in the amount of advice and structure they provide you. Psychoanalysts and nondirective therapists play a passive role, while some other therapists offer specific advice about overcoming problems. Psychotherapists ordinarily do not resent a prospective patient or client's asking them about what type of treatment approach they plan to use in their situation. Your feelings should be taken into account in selecting an approach to therapy.

Comprehensive discussion about counseling and psychotherapy falls outside the scope of this book; however, one crucial point about psychotherapy as an approach to overcoming emotional disturbance requires emphasis. Psychotherapy is a time-consuming and painstaking process, the results of which cannot be guaranteed. During the process of psychotherapy your defenses may be temporarily removed and the result can be painful. Personal change is serious business. There are some risks, but the reward of less discontentment and less disturbance is a powerful lure.

Psychotherapy Is Also for Normal People

Widespread is the misconception that only "crazy," "disturbed," or hopelessly malcontent people are candidates for psychotherapy. According to some well-documented research evidence, the opposite is more nearly correct. Normal, healthy people with specific conflicts and concerns derive more benefit from psychotherapy than do people with severe emotional disturbances. Therapists who claim remarkably high cure rates often select only reasonably healthy patients into their practice.

Counseling applied to emotionally healthy women for purposes of life planning was discussed in Chapter 4. Psychotherapy is a useful vehicle for gaining additional self-knowledge. Insights about your interpersonal relationships and the sources of your conflicts and concerns are sometimes forthcoming from psychotherapy. Sensitivity and encounter groups also provide an opportunity to acquire insight, but in these groups the insights come more from peers than from the therapist or group leader. Here is a sampling of the kinds of questions some emotionally healthy women have sought answers to in psychotherapy. Definitive answers are never guaranteed, but the emotional and intellectual experience of examining your own feelings is worthwhile to many women.

> I wonder if I've been too submissive in my relationships with my husband.

Am I too concerned about my looks and my age?

Why is it that I always pick friends who are better looking than myself?

Is it normal to think that my husband can never be as close to me as my father is?

Is it weird to be mad at your children for interfering with your career?

I get terribly anxious whenever I'm in a crowded room. What should I do about it?

Women who have undergone a successful experience in psychotherapy usually find new ways of looking at themselves. Many of the problems women face stem from society—other women and men included—not revamping their conceptions and stereotypes about women. Next we turn our attention to this issue.

NOTES

1. These six questions are based upon an analysis by Gerald M. Knox, "Mental Illness: When Someone Needs Help," in Charles A. Heidenreich, *Basic Readings in Behavior Disorders*, Berkeley, Calif., McCutchan Publishing Corp., 1969, pp. 229-236.
2. Abraham H. Maslow and Bela Mittelman, *Principles of Abnormal Psychology*, New York, Harper & Brothers, 1951, pp. 14-15.

Chapter 10

A NEW TAXONOMY FOR FEMALES

> *A witty woman is a treasure; a witty beauty is a power.*
>
> GEORGE MEREDITH
> *Diana of Crossways*

Accomplishment Is Masculine and Feminine

A SIMPLE misperception exists in our society about the relationship between sex and accomplishment. Looking underneath the rationalizations and other defenses of many people (including the well educated among their numbers), we find they regard accomplishment, achievement, and the acquisition of power and status as distinctly masculine attributes. Such stereotyped beliefs are based upon the following logic: Men are active and aggressive; women are passive and nonaggressive. Accomplishment and success require active and aggressive behavior, therefore it is a male attribute to rise to significant levels of accomplishment. Extending this reasoning, women with strong needs for accomplishment in the world outside the home are considered masculine. "Feminine" women prefer not to compete, according to this set of beliefs.

Origins of this simplistic notion about the relationship between sex and accomplishment are readily traced. Presumably the child-bearing and rearing functions of females in most early civilizations kept them close to home while males, unencumbered by pregnancy and nursing, were placed in the role of coping with the outside world in terms of hunting and fishing. Discussions about the different roles males and females play in various cultures are probably familiar to most readers; thus these anthropological debates need not be repeated here. One key point, however, merits attention. According to some anthropological studies relatively few societies attempt to keep women at home. Child rearing is thus regarded as a full-time occupation in only some societies.

Freudian psychology, including that of his disciples, provided modern-day reinforcement of the belief that women of accomplishment have strong masculine tendencies. Orthodox psychoanalytic theory contends that the pursuit of an intellectual career is simply a sublimation of "penis envy." (According to this concept, girls at an unconscious level really would like to have a penis of their own. Most girls overcome these feelings. Those unable to overcome these feelings recognize that anatomy cannot be reversed. As a substitute for the real thing they pursue a masculine career.) Many males still equate female drives for achievement as symptoms of distorted psychosexual development. Nurses in one mental hospital who proposed significant changes in the operations of the hospital were classified as "phallic-aggressive" by psychiatrists.[1] Freudian notions about women, of course, have been subject to bitter attack by intellectual leaders of the women's liberation movement.

Curiously, research evidence gathered in the 1950's also suggested that achievement is largely a masculine attribute. David McClelland, the psychologist most closely associated with developing present-day knowledge about the "achievement need," analyzed different manifestations of this need in females and males. Men, in his studies, expressed their achievement needs primarily through intelligence and leadership capacity. Women expressed their achievement needs through social acceptability. Girls strive to achieve if others expect it of them, but unguided by the influence of other people they exhibit only modest levels of achievement motivation.[2] Cultural pressures exerted on girls (particularly in the era in which these studies were conducted) undoubtedly had a suppressing effect upon their achievement motivation.

In sum, traditional thinking suggests that women who pursue career accomplishment are more masculine than feminine. Feminist thinking argues that the pursuit of accomplishment tells us nothing about a woman's psychosexual development. Paradoxically, both camps are expressing half-truths. An imperfect relationship exists between accomplishment and sexual orientation; accomplishment can be a masculine or feminine attribute. Masculine men vary considerably in how much they accomplish or even want to accomplish; some masculine men are lazy, some are ambitious. Feminine women also vary in their desires for accomplishment. Some feminine women accomplish very little, while others hold key positions in society. Some lesbians are achievement oriented; others give little thought to achievement. Some male homosexuals aspire toward high levels of accomplishment, while many others have limited aspirations in this area.

The Femininity and Accomplishment Indicator

Sexual orientation and accomplishment, expressed in the language of the behavioral scientist, are somewhat "independent" of each other. An imperfect relationship exists between these two facets of human behavior. Knowledge of a woman's sexual orientation does not accurately predict her drives for accomplishment; nor do her drives for success predict her femininity. The Femininity and Accomplishment Indicator shown in Figure 1 has been developed to illustrate that femininity and accomplishment come in many different combinations. Both key dimensions of women must be examined simultaneously to arrive at a better understanding of the relationship between psychosexual preferences and accomplishment.

Femininity is indicated on the vertical (up-and-down) axis. Low femininity (or masculinity) is found at the bottom of the axis. High femininity is indicated at the top of the axis. Average femininity would be placed in the middle. Women (and men) come in all different degrees of femininity. Feminine in the context used here is not synonymous with beauty, but does include appearance. Feminine, according to our definition, refers to charm, grace, poise, and both physical and psychological attractiveness. Femininity is in reality a composite of many overt and subtle characteristics. Nobody to my knowledge has conducted research on the extent to which femininity can reliably be measured, but it appears that reasonable agreement can be reached about what constitutes femininity. Each man or woman may have subjective preferences about who is an ideally feminine women, but some consensus probably exists about whether or not a given women should be de-

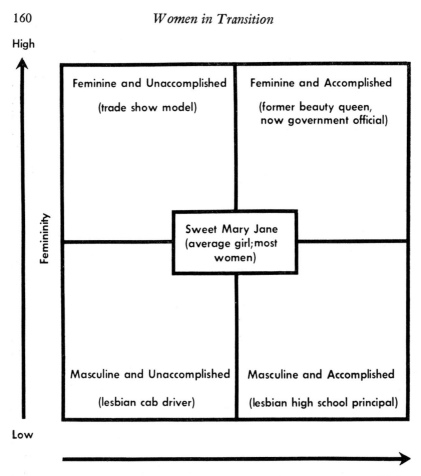

High

Femininity

Low

Low   Accomplishment   High

Figure 1. The Femininity and Accomplishment Indicator.

scribed as feminine.

Accomplishment is indicated across the horizontal axis of the Femininity and Accomplishment Indicator. Low accomplishment is placed on the left side of the axis; medium accomplishment is placed in the middle; the right side is reserved for high accomplishment. Accomplishment in the context used here refers to achieving goals that society thinks are worthwhile, or at least difficult and complex. File clerks, busgirls, fruit pickers, and women whose major preoccupation in life involves grooming themselves exemplify women of low accomplishment. Fashion editors, bank officers, novelists, hospital administrators, attorneys, child psychologists, and college professors typify women of high accomplishment. Accomplishment, like femininity, is also an end-product dimension of behavior. Factors such as intelligence, education, ambition, and opportunity facilitate accomplishment.

Women can be placed at almost any point on the Femininity and Accomplishment Indicator. Next we will study five key points on the Indicator, each characterizing the femininity and accomplishment pattern of different women.

Feminine and Unaccomplished

Feminine women with low needs for accomplishment are placed in the upper left-hand corner of the Indicator. When choosing a career or job they gravitate towards occupations that are sterotypically female but low in intellectual accomplishment. Carhops, cocktail waitresses, and call girls (jobs where pay is more dependent upon feminine charm than occupational skills) are examples of feminine and unaccomplished women. Women in this category are often highly valued by men. Such women represent no threat to male egos. Women in this category fall neatly into the "beautiful but dumb" and "magnificient babe" sterotypes. Feminine and unaccomplished women are roughly analogous to male construction workers. Their peak earning years occur when they are young and strong. Age quickly deteriorates feminine and unaccomplished women because much of their attractiveness to other people (and quite often themselves) is dependent upon physical appearance. Because of this factor, these women invest considerable time and money in personal grooming.

Feminine and unaccomplished women infrequently suffer from the housewife syndrome. Most of their needs for accomplishment can be met in the home. Jobs and formal education are valued primarily as in effective way of meeting a husband. Daughters of these women are taught intimate secrets of housewifery. A commercial artist with a feminine but unaccomplished mother recounts the following: "I can never forget my mother telling me to get all the egg off from forks. She said, 'How can you expect to keep a good husband if you leave egg on the fork?' "

Sons of these women are encouraged toward activities and interests culture defines as masculine, and discouraged from feminine activities. Sex-role differentiation is rarely a problem for children of feminine and unaccomplished women because their mother and father usually carry out distinctly different occupational roles. Additionally, they perceive women as being "feminine" and men as "masculine."

Masculine and Unaccomplished

Bottom left on the Indicator is the woman with atypical psychosexual development and low occupational accomplishment. Many masculine and unaccomplished women were found among the ranks of enlisted personnel in the Women's Army Corps in the second world war and in the immediately following postwar period. Masculine women with limited aspirations (or ability) face difficult adjustment problems. Most people, male and female, in their socioeconomic class have hostile attitudes toward masculine-appearing women, whether or not they are in fact lesbians. Masculine-appearing women, however heterosexual in preference, find male companionship in scant supply.

Women unfortunate enough to qualify for placement in the masculine and unaccomplished quadrant of the Indicator thus face limited opportunity for high levels of satisfaction in life. Full-time homemaking, even when available to them, is not a prized role in terms of their personal value system. Simultaneously, they have only a modest career orientation. Furthermore, lasting friendships are difficult for them to achieve because they are subject to overt and covert rejection from both males and females.

Masculine and Accomplished

Women placed on the bottom right-hand corner of the Femininity and Accomplishment Indicator provide support the Freudian notion of the successful woman with masculine strivings. Perhaps it is these women, more than Freud, who are responsible for the widely accepted stereotype that women of accomplishment are unfeminine or masculine. Women in this category often fit the stereotype of the man-tailored and unemotional woman. Frequently they are competitive with and hostile toward men. Despite these underlying attitudes many masculine and accomplished women work effectively with males. Compassion toward the problems of female employees is rarely their forte and they favor authoritarian leadership practices.

Many masculine and accomplished women hold significant positions in business and government. These include army officer, magazine editor, chief of nursing, high school principal, women's liberation leader (note carefully, not all), and even head of government. Among the positive traits found in such women are high intelligence, energy, and enthusiasm. Many of these women are homosexual or bisexual, but the majority are probably heterosexual.

Rarely do these women allow themselves to fall prey to the housewife syndrome. Marriage and child rearing represent minimum interference with their careers. High-masculine, high-accomplishment women tend to make satisfactory life companions for men who are similarly committed to their own careers. Motherhood, however, usually represents their Achilles' heel, because they have difficulty identifying with children and their problems.

Sweet Mary Jane

Here is the average, pleasant, wholesome, normal, ordinary, uncomplicated, wife, mother, lover, secretary, or school teacher. She is found on Elm Street in Dubuque, Iowa; on Tremont Avenue in the Bronx, New York; and on Vista Boulevard in El Paso, Texas. Ethnic backgrounds of these women include, among many others, Italian, Jewish, Swedish, German, and Polish.

Women placed at midpoint on the Femininity-Accomplishment Indicator also make up the average range on most surveys. They are the women whom product designers attempt to please. Many of them are statistically the typical suburbanite—two years of college, two and one half children, with a middle-manager, junior executive husband. Sweet Mary Janes are rarely extreme in any significant category of human behavior. Most of these women have had some kind of occupational experience but it is subordinate to their primary role of homemaker. Large proportions of these women are found among the contented homemakers discussed in Chapter 8. Discontentment and emotional disturbance tend to be lower among women in this average category than among women placed at the other four key points on the Indicator.

Feminine and Accomplished

Women of alluring femininity and outstanding accomplishment are located at the upper right-hand corner of the Indicator. The feminine and accomplished woman represents the ideal to many men and women. She is charming, independent in her thinking, and achieves positive results in most activities she undertakes. "Self-fulfilled" is a term that can be meaningfully applied to many of these women. Among them are public relations executives, authors, show business producers, university administrators, and cosmetic company executives. Several women's liberation leaders appear to fall into the Feminine and Accomplished category. Perhaps in the future more of these women will occupy such traditional male positions as manufacturing executive or union leader. Many of these women, however, would reject such roles due to lack of interest on their part.

Feminine and accomplished women rate at the positive end of the scale on most dimensions of human behavior. Intelligence, resourcefulness, ambition, and sensitivity toward people are among their key psychological characteristics. Their superiority as people even spills over into the sexual realm. Older studies by Maslow indicate that independent and assertive women experience more total sexual enjoyment than to their more passive and dependent counterparts.[3] Many feminine and accomplished women sympathize with the demands of women's liberationists, but most have never required a movement to achieve their personal goals. Women in this category have already accomplished the transition in life they are seeking.

If forced by circumstances to occupy a full-time homemaker role most of these women would experience the housewife syndrome. Guarding against such a reality, they recognize the value of a multiple role in society and have elected to be both homemaker and career woman. Their life is complex and demanding, but rewarding. They represent superb models of accomplishment and interpersonal skills for their children. Also, they place less time demands upon their husbands because of serious commitments to their own interests. Self-confidence and an absence of male-supremacy attitudes are vital attributes for the husband of a feminine and accomplished woman. Weaker males are threatened by these women and thus are at a competitive disadvantage in the marital relationship. Feminine and accomplished women have been known to have more friends and earn higher incomes than their husbands.

Where Do You Fit on the Indicator?

Five vignettes have been presented about women at key points on the Femininity and Accomplishment Indicator. Relationships between sex and accomplishment have been described in two dimensions rather than the conventional one-dimensional approach. The term "dimension" is chosen with considerable thought. Femininity versus masculinity and low accomplishment versus high accomplishment are analogous to height. People are characterized as being short or tall, but these are really only points on a scale.

Figure 2 offers you an opportunity to plot your proper place on the combined dimensions of femininity and accomplishment. Self-ratings, assuredly, can be inaccurate and this is not a diagnostic instrument of any scientific precision. Placing yourself on the Femininity and Accomplishment Indicator is simply intended as a vehicle for you to ask questions about yourself in a systematic manner.

First rate yourself on the dimension of femininity. How feminine am I? Where do I rate on a scale of one (kind of masculine) to five (very feminine and attractive). Husbands, friends, and surprisingly, adolescent children might help you verify your own rating here. Assume that Woman A rates herself as midway between three and four on femininity (essentially she feels above average in this regard). She draws a dotted line extending out to the right on the Work Sheet.

Second, rate yourself on a one-to-five scale of accomplishment. Objectivity is easier to achieve here than in rating yourself on femininity. Professional-level and managerial occupations should rate between four and five, particularly if you are performing effectively in such a position. Semiprofessional-level occupations such as primary and secondary school teaching, nursing, insurance claims adjusting, and dietician should rate between three and four, depending upon the level of competency. Effective homemaking should rate around average—between two and three. This rating represents a personal judgment on the author's part. Dr. Benjamin

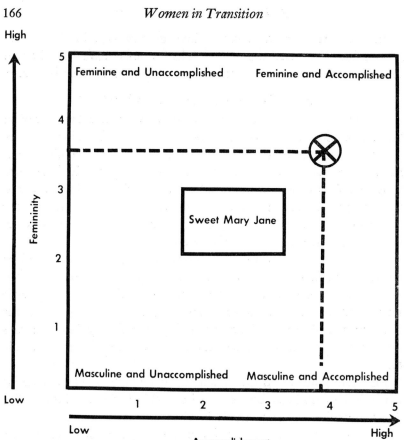

Figure 2. The Femininity and Accomplishment Indicator—Work Sheet.
Note: Illustrative woman rates herself midway between 3 and 4 on femininity, and almost 4 on accomplishment. She thus falls approximately into the Feminine and Accomplished zone.

Spock might rate homemaking five, while a militant feminist might rate it one. Occupational activities at the one and two levels include file clerk, beauty parlor attendant (not hair stylist), food checker in supermarket, night clerk in motel, and production worker.

Accomplishment can also come through community activities and in some situations, hobbies. Arrive at your rating by comparing your accomplishment to that of others. For example, if you are president of the local school board, your rating would be five. If you stuff envelopes for charity drives, your accomplishment level might be one or two in this area.

Woman A is a computer programming supervisor, and a college graduate with a math major. She rates her accomplishment level as "almost four." A line is drawn vertically from that point on the bottom line. According to her self-image she is "a little more feminine than average" and thus rates herself between three and four on femininity. A dotted line is then drawn from this point to the right. Where the two lines (femininity and accomplishment) intersect a circle is drawn. Woman A's position on the Indicator is approaching the Feminine and Accomplished zone, and definitely beyond the Sweet Mary Jane zone.

Should you be dissatisfied with your placement on the Femininity-Accomplishment Indicator, it may be time to begin your transition toward a more favorable point. Movement in such a direction will require self-discipline and self-liberation.

NOTES

1. Jay Schulman, *Remaking an Organization: Innovation in a Specialized Psychiatric Hospital,* Albany, State University of New York Press, 1969, as reported in a review by Matthew B. Miles in *Contemporary Psychology, 15:556,* (No. 9) 1970.
2. Reported in Edwin C. Lewis, *Developing Woman's Potential,* Ames, Iowa State University Press, pp. 75, 278.
3. Reported in Betty Friedan, *The Feminine Mystique,* New York, Dell, 1970, pp. 299-305.

Chapter 11

TOWARD SELF-LIBERATION

The woman that deliberates is lost.

JOSEPH ADDISON
Cato, Act IV, Scene 1

What Is Self-Liberation?

"SELF-LIBERATION" implies that it is your responsibility to liberate yourself. If you feel trapped as a housewife you have to untrap yourself. You supply the motivational force to make real the upward transition this book has been about. Practically all help in psychological areas is self-help. Unless you are committed to self-improvement other people cannot help you.

Self-liberation does not imply that nobody can help you; psychiatrists do help patients, teachers do help students, counselors do help clients, trainers do help trainees. The efforts of all these helpers, however, are virtually wasted unless the person being helped wants to be helped. Life circumstances also have to be suitable for change to take place. If your family is worried about economic survival and your husband is violently opposed to your making a positive transition, self-liberation looks doubtful.

How to Make the Transition

Assume that self-liberation, self-development, self-fulfillment, or self-realization is what you really want and also that life circumstances do not prevent you from achieving these goals. Next are some actions to take (or avoid) and attitudes to develop that will move you toward self-fulfillment and help you become a woman in transition. These twenty guidelines bring together all of the key points for personal growth mentioned in this book.

1. If you feel discontented, bored, lethargic, and that your talents

are being underutilized, admit that you have a problem.

> Myra Johnson feels this way but keeps looking for physical prob-
> lems that will explain these feelings. She has been to three different
> doctors in a frantic search for a physical explanation of her prob-
> lems. Until she accepts the fact that she may be experiencing the
> housewife syndrome, she cannot become a woman in transition.

2. Insure that some part of your normal day involves conversation with mature adults about topics other than homemaking in
general and child care in particular.

> Nancy Elms is a homemaker with three preschool children. Much
> of her day involves conversing with children or hearing children's
> television programs. Her husband travels frequently and she is new
> to her community. Gradually she begins to relate to adults as if they
> were children and her confidence in talking about topics other than
> child rearing begins to diminish.
> Recognizing her problem, she made an effort to build a friend-
> ship with a woman who had no children. Her new friend and she
> had dinner or lunch together once per week and agreed not to talk
> about children or anything related to homemaking during their en-
> counter. Nancy gradually felt less engulfed by the world of chil-
> dren.

3. Suggest to your husband (and perhaps your children) that
they should tell you about it when you do something exceptionally
well.

> Doris McKenzie works diligently at her homemaking and com-
> munity responsibilities yet nobody offers her praise. Finally, recog-
> nizing her normal need for praise, she confronted her husband:
> "Jim, if you treated your employees like you treat me, you'd have a
> serious turnover problem. Gifts at holidays and birthdays are not
> enough. I'd like you to tell me when you think I've done some-
> thing very good." Jim profited from this insight and began to pay
> his wife appropriate compliments. Doris now feels more appreciated
> and thus receives a few more satisfactions from homemaking.

4. Take that big first step on the road toward self-fulfillment
(if you haven't already done it). Chances are that you are bright
enough and young enough to find more satisfaction in life. Courage,
however, is needed to get started.

> Louise Collins felt she was permanently locked into the full-time
> homemaker's role. Her underlying fear was that at age forty-one

she was too old to acquire new skills. "The only full time job I've ever had is being a housewife." One night she finally sat down and began to clarify her thoughts about what she would like to do in life. Two years later she is a media specialist in a local high school.

5. Acquire knowledge about your own capabilities and potentials. Many women have aptitudes they never realized.

Mary Carvell has always enjoyed and performed well at games such as bridge, checkers, and chess. She asked herself and her husband (a personnel manager), "How could my interest in games be useful in business?" Mary's husband arranged for her to take a computer-programming aptitude test. Her score fell into the "A" range. Today she is a computer programmer and is a likely candidate for the next managerial position within her department.

6. Give some thought to joining a women's liberation group as one possible vehicle for self-growth.

Sally Wickam commented, "I thought Women's Lib members were a bunch of rabble-rousers and kooks. Finally a friend dragged me to a consciousness-raising session. Actually it was quite good. Those gals are trying to get decent day care facilities in our town. The group discussions helped me better understand my attitudes toward men."

7. If your husband (or any close male companion) is a successful, committed person, develop some commitments and interests of your own.

Mary Ellen Coffey is married to the Director of Research in one section of a university. He works sixty hours per week and wishes he could find more hours to work. Mary Ellen, in self-defense, became engrossed in life insurance sales. She is now the one who is sometimes too busy for social life. Mary Ellen and her husband have developed more respect for each other's way of life and their marriage has improved.

8. If you feel competitive toward your friends, husband, or children, find an area of competition in which your chances of being successful are good.

Elizabeth Bartell resents the attention her husband receives from his role as a television announcer. To satisfy some of her competitive urges she encouraged her husband to take up skiing with her. On the basis of extra practice and natural skill, Elizabeth within one season surpassed her husband in skiing. She is now better able to accept her husband's notoriety because she outperforms him in one shared activity.

9. Strengthen your self-image by achieving goals that stretch your capability.

> Susan Strauss decided to become a world's expert on something. One day she hit upon the idea of studying the history of writing instruments (fountain pens, quill pens, pencils, and so forth). After two years of research she is ready to begin writing her manuscript, *A Natural History of Writing Instruments.* Says Susan, "I don't care about the royalties. What gives me a lift is that I'm now the world's leading authority on something that's interesting to me, and it took a lot of hard work to get there."

10. Develop a serious commitment to something besides yourself. The depth of your commitment is more important than the type of activity you choose.

> Mildred Parsons searched for something to which she could commit herself. She had tried taking courses, playing bridge, and part-time work as a teacher's assistant. None of these activities held her interest. Mildred decided to give her next activity a fair trial by developing proficiency in that activity before dropping it for another. She focused her attention on becoming a telephone respondent in a suicide prevention center. Mildred immersed herself in information about the causes and prevention of suicide. She learned to accept minor frustrations in the work as inevitable. Two years later Mildred still finds her work at the suicide prevention center personally rewarding and socially useful.

11. Practice habits of good mental health. This is a complex and difficult assignment, but the points mentioned in Chapter 4 are helpful guidelines. Not everybody has life circumstances that permit them to practice good mental health, but most people can benefit from these principles.

> Jeanne Bridgman does what she can to practice good mental health. Her friends and family would describe her as "well adjusted." Jeanne is a speech therapist, married, and has one child. She keeps in good physical shape through golf, skiing, and jogging. Jeanne feels she is average in appearance and less than brilliant, but she can accept these facets of herself. She is often impatient with people, but she accepts the fact that they are entitled to opinions and values different from hers. Jeanne maintains a close, confidential relationship with three people: her husband, best friend, and

mother. She expresses her opinion when asked, but avoids hurting other people's feelings. When Jeanne is tense or upset she does something constructive about it. She is serious about her work as a speech therapist and has some plans for further graduate study in her field. Jeanne finds outlet for her creative urges in oil painting. "I know I'm a terrible artist, but my painting is just for my own enjoyment."

12. Involve your husband in your plans for self-development. Without his cooperation, your progress will be hampered.

Joanne Sullivan decides that returning to school represents a good starting point in her road toward self-fulfillment. Laboratory work holds considerable appeal for her. She asks her husband, Phil, to investigate the demand for laboratory technicians in their area, the type of educational preparation necessary, and so on. Phil works diligently to obtain the information his wife needs. After a while he thinks it is his idea to send Joanne back to school. In the process he becomes enthusiastic about her plans and provides her the encouragement and assistance in homemaking chores she needs.

13. Free more time for self-improvement by applying more systematic work habits to homemaking responsibilities. For example, devote more time to planning errands and chores before actually doing them.

Bonnie Irwin took a long hard look at why she performed certain household tasks. Among her time-saving discoveries were these: (1) Washing her car in the spring wasted time because leaving the car out in the rain worked just as well as a car wash. (2) Body heat takes the wrinkles out of her children's polo shirts, making ironing them superfluous. (3) Her ten-year-old daughter enjoyed clearing the table after dinner. (4) Nobody in her house cared if she only washed the windows once or twice per year. These "time-savers," combined with better planning of her housework, gave Bonnie more time for self-development.

14. If child-rearing responsibilities (and your own guilt feelings) keep you home, take positive steps to prevent becoming obsolete.

Pat Kramer gave birth to twins two years after her first child was born. Prior to child rearing, Pat was an advertising copy writer. She now devotes three hours per week—all the time she can spare—to writing advertising copy without pay for church and civic groups. She also maintains a file of advertising ideas for well-known products. Pat hopes to use these when she someday returns to the world of advertising. She attempts to keep abreast of the advertising field by phone conversations with old business associates and by studying advertisements in magazines.

15. Don't expect to find self-fulfillment through an extramarital affair. That places too much burden on sex and love. (I am not saying affairs have no value.)

> Lois Roth provides this observation about a former affair: "No question my relationship with him put some needed spark in my life. Meeting for lunch, seeing him when my husband was out of town was a real adventure. But hell, I still wanted to become something more than a housewife. I didn't give up my college program just because I didn't feel lonely anymore. That wasn't why I started back to college in the first place."

16. Don't feel abnormal, strange or old-fashioned if you happen to be contented with full-time homemaking. If your goals in life are to be a superb mother, wife, and housekeeper, stay right where you are. Self-fulfillment comes from reaching your goal in life, even if that goal is homemaking.

> Janice Duffy has four children and is married to a surgeon. During the past several years she began to wonder why she didn't experience all the problems homemakers were supposed to have. She feels that with her husband's hectic schedule, the large house, and four children, there is no way for her to manage a career outside the home. "I like what I'm doing. It keeps me going all the time. I don't want my life to be any more complicated."

17. Should you feel that your path to self-fulfillment is blocked by an overload of personal concerns and worries, seek professional help.

> Eleanor Parks tried several different approaches to self-development in order to combat the housewife syndrome. None of these activities brought her the satisfaction she was seeking. Finally she gravitated toward psychotherapy as an approach to her problems. Psychotherapy helped her resolve a key underlying personal conflict. She was afraid to become successful in anything but housework because of her mother's experience with her father. Eleanor's father had vehement attitudes about "the woman's place being in the home." Any attempts by her mother to find satisfactions outside the house were met with verbal and sometimes physical resistance by the father. Eleanor, underneath, feared that if she developed serious interests outside the home her husband would develop

the same attitudes toward her that her father had toward her mother. Psychotherapy, combined with open discussion with her husband about this topic, helped Eleanor overcome her roadblock to personal fulfillment.

18. Feel free to accomplish what you want to in life without worrying about your femininity. Women can be both feminine *and* accomplished.

> Elaine Marcel placed second in the Miss Chicago beauty contest at age eighteen. Upon graduation from Northwestern University she began work in a Chicago bank as a management trainee. Eight years later she is married, has one child, and is also a vice president of personnel at the same bank. Elaine's secretary describes her as a "superwoman." She is in demand as a luncheon companion both for her feminine charm and her stimulating ideas. Elaine typifies the new motif in interesting women.

19. Remember that self-fulfillment is a continuing process. The woman in transition never stops growing. You can lessen your discontents and increase your satisfactions in life, but no woman's situation is perfect.

> Barbara Collier is the president of an advertising agency and a wife and mother. Asked about the problems she encounters in her dual career, she states: "Many people think I lead about the coolest life possible. I have recognition, money, fun, and a good husband. But you know I'm in a damn rat race. It would only take the loss of one or two big clients and our business would go under. Many days I don't even have time for lunch. It's not easy being a wife, mother, and company president, but I wouldn't give up this three-ring circus for anything."

20. Other women who have made the transition from discontentment to a more rewarding life had to start somewhere. Take that first step and keep going. The journey toward self-fulfillment is one of life's most exciting adventures.

INDEX